T. Coleman

PRAYER

PRAYER

By Roger Forster

British Library Cataloguing-in-Publication Data

A catalogue record for this book is available from the British Library

ISBN 1-85078-469-8

Cover design by Diane Bainbridge
Printed in Great Britain by
Cox & Wyman Ltd., Reading

Dedication

PRAYER

This book is dedicated to Faith, my wife, who not only lives what I teach here but has inspired me to pursue more intensely a life in God's life. She has also enhanced these pages by contributing the fifth chapter.

Contents

Dedication		v
Introduction		ix
1.	Why Must We Pray?	1
2.	How Must We Pray?	16
3.	The Lord's Prayer	26
4.	Prophetic Prayer	63
5.	Word and Prayer	86
6.	Praying 'Bible Prayers'	106
7.	Praying in the Breath of God	114
8.	Pressures in Prayer	131
9.	Passionate Prayer	141

Introduction

God is a social God, a bunch of relationships, Father, Son and Holy Spirit. He lives in these relationships. In fact, as the Holy Spirit is God's breath, or breathing, so the Son of God is the Father's eternal life according to 1 John 1:2, and the Son's life is given by the Father (John 5:26).

It is not surprising, therefore, that the Christian life is equally born out of our relationship with the Father, through the Son, by the Spirit. Everything in the Christian life comes out of fellowship with Jesus. What kind of relationship, or what kind of fellowship exists without communication? That communication is not simply 'prayer' or 'a prayer' but it is 'praying without ceasing', which is just another way of saying 'living in God's breath'. This book is written in the conviction that this is not only a possibility, but a necessity.

I would make a plea to the reader that when encountering a biblical allusion which is not familiar, he or she would be kind enough to look up the verses in the Scriptures. It is in this way that some of the finer points of exegesis will be appreciated; appreciation strengthens conviction and conviction, in turn, strengthens practice as the beauty of God's truth leads to worship.

It was one of Watchman Nee's younger colleagues – in fact, one of the last four he sent away from the persecution while he himself stayed with the flock of believers in China

– who once said to me that he had in his youth puzzled over Paul's statement that we should pray without ceasing. But as he got older, he assured me, he began to understand. He had begun to experience the truth of it, as he daily lived in Jesus' life and breathed his breath. May the Lord who breathed on the Apostles in the upper room so share his life with us increasingly, (and hopefully with the help of the chapters of this book), so that we may be aware that we too are sent in the power of the Holy Spirit to give life and forgiveness to a dying, unforgiven and peaceless world (John 20).

1

Why Must We Pray?

There is nothing more human than prayer. When we look into the heart of God we find that his purpose for humankind before the world ever began was that we should have communion with each other and with him. It is only when we pray that we are truly human because it is only as we pray that we can truly discover, get to know and commune with God. Prayer is our very life-breath as humans. If life is not shared with someone it is dead: 'This is eternal life, that they may know You, the only true God' (John 17:3).

Living day by day requires that we interact and have relationships with other people. We need to talk together because it is as we talk that relationships develop. If we never communicate with anyone else we are not really living. If we never communicate with God we are not fulfilling what it means to be human; we are not reaching our potential as sharers in the divine life, the great destiny that God has always had in his heart for us. Life that lasts forever and does not die is a life spent communicating with God and sharing with one another as we get to know him both individually *and* corporately. Thus the Christian life subsists in prayer.

The Apostle Paul encourages us to 'pray without ceasing' (1 Thessalonians 5:17). This certainly does not mean that there is no place for 'seasons', 'sessions' or 'times' of prayer. Some people seem to think that to pray without ceasing means to dream along and hope that you are in touch with God and thus do without a specific time to sit down and talk to him. That is not true. Jesus had times of prayer, as we see if we look at Luke 11:1. However, when he had finished his time of prayer, he was still talking to the Father inwardly in his heart. It is very exciting to realise at the end of the day that everything you have been doing has been in the sight of the Lord. In every moment, in every circumstance, you have been turning to him, not necessarily using conscious thoughts, but just being open to him, rather like a friend who is so familiar that you don't always need to use words to communicate. That is how Paul can enjoin us to 'pray without ceasing', but this does not exclude the times we set aside particularly to spend with the Father.

Corporate times of prayer are also important. When we pray together we stimulate each other and because we are part of the same body (Romans 12:5) we function better in co-operation. We tend to learn best when we learn with others. Similarly, we often pray most effectively when we pray with others. It is when we come together in agreement that we find more power in our prayers (Matthew 18:19).

So, as we look more deeply into these areas we shall, hopefully, find out more about what it means to be truly human, truly Christian, truly divine images and truly a reflection of what God intended his church to be. This involves both praying on our own and in a group.

But why should we pray?

Communication

The earliest mention of human beings in the Bible is in Genesis 1:26: 'Let *Us* make man in Our image, according to Our likeness.' From this statement we learn something about God and something about humans made in his image. God is a God who talks, reflects and shares within the community of the Trinity. Within the union of the Godhead Father, Son and Holy Spirit are constantly communicating with one another, a wonderful Triune God! Thus prayer, divine communication, starts in the Trinity. The Father talks to the Son, the Son asks the Spirit, the Spirit puts it back to the Father and so on in an eternal interaction of love.

Human beings are made in God's image. Thus we too need to communicate. This is where prayer starts: 'Let *Us* make man in *Our image!*' We talk to God because he talks. John 1:1 says 'In the beginning was the Word' – not 'truth' or 'holiness' but 'the Word'. God speaks. That is why he likes us to talk to him: it is the first reflection of who he is.

God goes on to say 'and let them rule …' (Genesis 1:26) because God is also a God who rules and has dominion and his will gets done! But before we can 'rule and subdue the earth', before we can do the job we were commissioned by God to do, we have to begin by imitating and following God's first revealed characteristic – communication by prayer. We have to pray because we are made in God's image and it is part of our creatorial function. We are meant to communicate because God is a communicating God. There is a discipline in silence, but there is no discipline in non-communication.

When God speaks to Job and says, 'Who is this that dark-
ens counsel by words without knowledge? Now gird up
your loins like a man, and I will ask you, and you instruct
Me!' (Job 38:2–3) he is teasing Job. After all, if we take ourselves too seriously when we suffer, we tend to suffer twice
as much. If we are able to laugh at ourselves we alleviate
some of the pain. It is as if the Lord is saying to Job, 'Come
along now, you are acting like a growling animal! Talk properly with me like a man!' 'Gird up your loins!' is like 'Stand
on your feet!' This is one of the most important things about
human beings: we can stand on our feet; we are bipeds. We
are the only creatures who have been made able to stand, to
look up, to talk face-to-face. That is how we talk to God and
to one another. We were made to be talking animals. No
other animals talk – even the communicative ability of the
highly intelligent dolphin could not be called 'speech'. Only
humans have mouths that can articulate. The major part of
humankind's thinking is done through words and if we
were not able to speak we would not be so able to articulate ideas, concepts, or any of the deep things in our spirits.
Therefore talking to God, communication, is the beginning
of being 'like' God.

Communion

God's desire for humankind was not only that we would
communicate but that we would have communion with
him. That peaceful communion was broken in the Garden
of Eden:

They heard the sound of the Lord God walking in the garden in the cool of the day, and the man and his wife hid themselves from the presence of the Lord God among the trees of the garden. Then the Lord God called to the man, and said to him, 'Where are you?' (Genesis 3:8–9).

God was seeking to talk to Adam and Eve. We need to learn to pray and respond to God because he is still saying to us, 'Where are you?'

We would not want to pray or break out of the defensive 'castles' that we build around ourselves to keep people out if God was not constantly seeking us. He is trying to have communion with us and that is why we want to communicate back! Even when we do not quite know how to turn to God, or where to find him, it is the very fact that he is seeking us that ensures we have desire for him in our hearts. The psalmist sounds as if he wants to hide from God:

Where can I go from Your Spirit? Or where can I flee from Your presence? If I ascend to heaven, You are there; if I make my bed in Sheol, behold, You are there. If I take the wings of the dawn, if I dwell in the remotest part of the sea, even there Your hand will lead me, and Your right hand will lay hold of me (Psalm 139:7–10).

His words reflect awareness that God is 'after him'. Those who say 'Where is God?' in an attempt to disprove him do not seem to realise that the question itself implies some indication of his existence – otherwise why look for him in the first place? God is after us, and the fact that he is seeking us

is a great hope, the very means of bringing us into communion with him.

In Genesis we see God at the very beginning of
humankind's history, walking with humankind in the garden. That communion is brought to perfection in John 17,
where Jesus demonstrates his communion with his Father in
prayer. There is something very wonderful about this. In
John 17:3–8 the Lord says to his Father:

> This is eternal life, that *they* may know You, the only true God,
> and Jesus Christ whom You have sent. I glorified You on the
> earth, having accomplished the work which You have given
> Me to do. Now, Father, glorify Me together with Yourself, with
> the glory which I had with You before the world was. I have
> manifested Your name to *the men whom You gave Me* out of the
> world; *they* were Yours and You gave *them* to Me, and *they* have
> kept Your word. Now *they* have come to know that everything
> You have given Me is from You; for the words which You gave
> Me I have given to *them*; and *they* received them and truly
> understood that I came forth from You, and *they* believed that
> You sent Me.

Can you picture this incredible scene? In the upper room,
where the disciples were gathered for their last farewell with
the Lord, they hear him talking to his Father. As he speaks
it is as though he is reaching out his arms and pulling them
into the conversation. He is talking about them! They don't
say anything – it is too awe-inspiring. They are witnessing
the Father and the Son in communion and as they interact
together the disciples are drawn into the deepest and most

intimate place of relationship within the Godhead: the very heartbeat of God. As we get closer to our Lord Jesus he takes us nearer to the heart of God. And we in turn go deeper and deeper into their communion until we find that the energy of God's communion begins to overtake us. This is what Paul meant when he wrote 'the Spirit Himself intercedes for us with groanings too deep for words' (Romans 8:26). The Holy Spirit takes the mind of God and begins to put it inside us because we have been listening to God's heart, getting caught up in his kind of praying. When that happens we know we are beginning to pray about the right things! Communion with God is one reason we must pray. Communion is essential if we want to get into that wonderful place at the heart of the universe where we can listen to Father and Son sharing together and be drawn into that same life of prayer.

Command

We should pray because we are commanded to! Jesus tells us to 'pray and not give up' (Luke 18:1–8). He is not necessarily saying 'pray without ceasing', as Paul does, but he does mean that we ought to feel able to bring to God in prayer every little thing that comes up in our lives. Moreover, we should never grow weary until we receive an answer.

Paul also exhorts us in these same terms: 'Rejoice always'; 'Pray without ceasing'; 'In everything give thanks!'; 'Do not quench the Spirit' (1 Thessalonians 5:16–19). We are commanded to pray and not give up! Jesus thought it was important; Paul thought it was important. If we are constantly giving thanks and rejoicing we will find it easier to pray without ceasing! Paul often puts prayer and thanksgiving together in his letters because when we don't take God's goodness for granted but remain thankful for all that he gives us this naturally flows out in prayer to him. Romans 1:21 warns us that the product of an ungrateful heart is foolishness and ungodliness. It is as we remain thankful that we remain prayerful.

Co-operation

'God does nothing,' said John Wesley, 'except by prayer.' We may be inclined to think this an overstatement – it is obviously true that God keeps the whole universe running without anybody praying and asking him to do it! But when it comes to extending his kingdom into all things he does not enforce this on his own initiative, regardless of our involvement! He seeks the co-operation of the section of humanity that he has redeemed and to whom he can entrust his work. God works co-operatively. He is not into do-it-yourself! Instead, he seeks to share with his people so that together we can get things done. Wesley was not wrong.

It is only as we pray that God co-operates with us to get his will done. That is why he taught us to pray 'Your kingdom come. Your will be done, on earth as it is in heaven' (Matthew 6:10). How is God going to get heavenly things done on earth if we do not pray? We must break out of passive theology that says that God will do what he likes whenever, wherever, whether we pray about it or not. He won't! He chooses to work together with his children. He does not break in and make his children do things they don't want to do! Instead, he asks us to pray so that we can do things together. The Lord will have ideas that he will drop into our hearts and we will have some that we can offer up to him! The initiative may come from God, or it may be ours, but we work together. We are working not so much *for* God as *with* him! Amos says, 'Surely the Lord God does nothing unless He reveals His secret counsel to His servants the prophets' (Amos 3:7). Prophets pray or preach what they receive from God. No wonder God does little if the church does not pray, listen and respond!

Moses actually changed God's mind through prayer (Exodus 32:11–14). This is possible. Moses turned to the Lord and said:

O Lord, why does Your anger burn against Your people whom You have brought out from the land of Egypt with great power and with a mighty hand? Why should the Egyptians speak, saying, 'With evil intent He brought them out to kill them in the mountains and to destroy them from the face of the earth'? Turn from Your burning anger and change Your mind about doing harm to Your people. Remember Abraham, Isaac, and Israel.

God knew, of course, that he had brought Israel out of Egypt with a mighty hand. He didn't need to be reminded. God knew that the Egyptians would say he had allowed his people to be destroyed in the wilderness. But he needed somebody to take up the point with him! God works through co-operation. We must take up what we know about God in his presence so that he can see that we are sharing in who he is and what he does. Moses' prayer showed extraordinary insight into the character of God. He knew that God did not want to give up on his people. He knew that God wanted to vindicate them before the nations. He knew that in his anger the Lord would remember mercy, relent, and not carry out his threat of destruction. So Moses reminded God that he is merciful and showed God that he wanted to co-operate with him in that mercy. As we pray like this God is achieving his ultimate purpose of getting us to understand and work together with him. Then he can act according to his will.

Don't be afraid that this limits God's power – it is simply the way he has chosen to run the universe. It is his desire to move in conjunction with his people. God is not love for his own sake. Love is for the other person. God is love for the creatures that he has made. How could it be otherwise? And so God heard Moses' prayer and instead of destroying the children of Israel he enabled them to go on travelling in the desert for another thirty-eight years.

Compassion

In Matthew 9:36–38 the Lord looked around at the people and saw them as sheep without a shepherd. He saw them lying down, distressed and under pressure, and because he was moved with compassion he called on his disciples to pray. 'Therefore beseech the Lord of the harvest to send out workers into His harvest,' he said. It was out of compassion for the 'lostness' of the people that Jesus prayed and encouraged his disciples to pray. Even if we do not care about praying for our own sakes we must keep praying for other people's sakes! Let compassion move you to pray for others and to see their needs. Pray because people need to be loved and because you love them and want them to be blessed. In James 4:2–3 the Lord's brother reminds us that we 'do not have because [we] do not ask', or if we do ask we ask wrongly, from wrong motives. Self-interest often gets in the way of our praying. It is far easier to pray believingly for someone else's problems than it is for our own. We can pray and have faith for healing for other people when we have very little faith for our own. Why? Because there is nothing more altruistic than praying for others out of compassion. We need to pray without self-interest, but with lots of compassion!

Continuation

We have to pray in order that we might continue with the Lord. If we do not pray we will not go on with God. In John 15 Jesus uses the magnificent description of himself as the 'vine' and his disciples as the branches. It is in this context that fruit is to be brought forth through pruning.

Jesus goes on to speak about the necessity of pruning so that there is 'much fruit' (John 15:2,8). The question is, what kind of fruit are we talking about? Most people would say that it is the life of Jesus in the believer, the fruit of the Spirit: love, joy, peace, patience, kindness, goodness, faithfulness, gentleness and self-control. However, the Apostle Paul had not yet written that! The 'fruit' is not just a general type of fruit of the life of Jesus working in a person; nor is it the fruit of evangelism, which is another kind of biblical fruit (bringing in the harvest is to bring in the fruit from evangelistic outreach – Matthew 9:37–38).

The best way to begin to interpret anything is to look into the text itself and see what it says. The fruit in this passage is already defined (John 15:7–8): 'If you abide in Me, and My words abide in you, ask whatever you wish, and it will be done for you. My Father is glorified by this, that you bear much fruit, and so prove to be My disciples.' What, then, is 'the fruit'? The fruit is: 'ask whatever you wish, and it will be done for you. My Father is glorified by this ...' The fruit is praying and receiving an answer, talking to God and seeing things change.

In case we are not quite convinced we can go to the only other place where there is a definition of the fruit, John 15:16. 'You did not choose Me but I chose you, and appointed you that you would go and bear fruit, and that your fruit would remain, so that whatever you ask of the Father in My name He may give to you.' This is the fruit – answered prayer!

If we do not keep asking and receiving answers then the pruning will cease and the branch will be taken away. The Lord's warning to us is clear. We need to go deeper and deeper in prayer, learning how to ask for something and how to receive it.

There is a story of an old country chapel. An erudite new preacher came to visit. He was given the opportunity to preach. Before he began he decided to pray. His prayer went all around the houses from the North Pole to the South Pole, explaining current world situations, applying complex theology to them, and quoting obscure Scriptures. The preacher was merely talking to God about things God knew already! While he was still in full flight the old farmer who locked and unlocked the chapel each week stood up at the back and called out: 'Here Mister! Why don't yer call 'im Father and ask 'im for summet?' This is what real praying is – calling on the Father and asking him for something. As our prayers are answered we grow up with God and are encouraged in our faith.

Jude 20–21 confirms this teaching: 'But you, beloved, building yourselves up on your most holy faith, praying in the Holy Spirit, keep yourselves in the love of God, waiting anxiously for the mercy of our Lord Jesus Christ to eternal life.' In other words, we build up and deepen our relationship with God as we continue to pray. We are going to be presented before his throne 'blameless, with great joy' (verse 24) because we have continued and kept going. How have we continued and kept going? By building ourselves up, praying in the Holy Spirit.

Confrontation

Finally, we must pray because praying is the way of doing battle, of confrontation, of driving the enemy out. There is an element of praying that is aggressive and war-like. Mark 11:22–23 tells us that if there are mountains in our way it is time that we commanded them to go and throw themselves into the sea: 'Truly I say to you, whoever says to this mountain, "Be taken up and cast into the sea," and does not doubt in his heart, but believes that what he says is going to happen, it will be granted him.' Jesus goes on to say (verse 24) 'all things for which you pray and ask, believe that you have received them, and they will be granted you'. Looking at a mountain and telling it to jump into the sea is prayer. If you face your problem, declare it out of the way, believing that it will go, that is praying, even though you are not directly addressing God. You are speaking towards the mountain, but you are actually talking to God, or talking before him in his presence.

Some people make a great deal of fuss about this. They say, 'You shouldn't really talk to the difficulties, you shouldn't address the devil or demons.' Nevertheless, casting out a demon is a type of praying! In the book of Jude we see that 'Michael the archangel, when he disputed with the devil and argued about the body of Moses, did not dare pronounce against him a railing judgment, but said, "The Lord rebuke you!"' (verse 9). There is not much to choose between saying, 'Lord, rebuke the devil!' and saying, 'Out, devil, in Jesus' name!' There is no real difference, for both prayers call on the Lord and appeal to God in his power to deal with the demon. Calling upon God to exert his power on our behalf is the only way to confront some situations. If you confront these situations without God there is no hope. Confront them with God and 'all things you ask in prayer, believing, you will receive' (Matthew 21:22). Alternatively, look at Ephesians 6:11–12:

> Put on the full armor of God, so that you will be able to stand firm against the schemes of the devil. For our struggle is not against flesh and blood, but against the rulers, against the powers, against the world forces of this darkness, against the spiritual forces of wickedness in the heavenly places.

We come into this realm and begin to attack only through prayer and speaking God's word. We know that the Father is listening as we declare Jesus' name to break the spiritual strongholds and as we take up the sword of the Spirit, which is the word of God. How? Through prayer! The answer, then, to our chapter's question is that we must pray to be truly human, to know God, to obey him, to co-operate with him, to bring forth fruit and to oppose evil.

2

How Must We Pray?

Christ-like prayer

Let us take a look at some of the different aspects of Jesus' prayer life, as examples to us.

1. Jesus heard from heaven

> Now when all the people were baptized, Jesus was also baptized, and while He was praying, heaven was opened, and the Holy Spirit descended upon Him in bodily form like a dove, and a voice came out of heaven, 'You are My beloved Son, in You I am well-pleased' (Luke 3:21–22).

Jesus prayed and heaven opened, he received the Holy Spirit, he heard the voice of the Father, and he knew the love of God: 'You are My beloved Son.' It is by prayer that heaven is opened and its resources made available to be received through the Spirit. Jesus spoke to his Father and heard his Father's voice. This is the way, if we follow Jesus, that we should pray, and so experience the Father's love and the Spirit's anointing.

2. Jesus was under authority

In Matthew 8:8–9 the centurion who has just had his servant healed from a distance says:

> Lord, I am not worthy for You to come under my roof, but just say the word, and my servant will be healed. For I also am a man under authority, with soldiers under me; and I say to this one, 'Go!' and he goes, and to another, 'Come!' and he comes, and to my slave, 'Do this!' and he does it.

When Jesus heard this he said 'Truly I say to you, I have not found such great faith with anyone in Israel' (Matthew 8:10). The model that the centurion presents to us is the model of getting answers to prayer. Jesus could heal the servant from a distance because the centurion perceived that he was someone who was *under* authority and therefore could *exert* authority.

Many people today do not believe in authority. They don't want to acknowledge God and therefore have no final authority. Similarly, the authority of a king, president, prime minister or headmaster is meaningless. There is the attitude: '*I* am not going to be under authority … but *you* can do what I tell you!' We try to exert authority without being under it. We tend to believe that the greatest achievement would be to possess authority and get our own way in everything so that nobody else can get theirs! But when we pray, in the very act of praying, we put ourselves under the authority of God. If we do not then we are not really pray-ing – that is why we do not see things happen.

James 4:7 says that when we are under the authority of God we can be given authority over the enemy: we can exert it, and the enemy flees. Jesus himself was under the authority of God, as the centurion recognised (Luke 7:8) – this is why his prayers were answered.

People who have never accepted that they are respon-sible to somebody else will never be given the privilege by God of having someone responsible to them. In fact it is very dangerous to come under the authority of somebody who is not responsible to anyone else. If, in the Christian life, we submit to anyone's authority, we must be convinced that he or she is submitted to the authority of God: in other words, that he or she prays.

3. Jesus ministered out of his prayer life

'I do nothing on My own initiative, but I speak these things as the Father taught Me' (John 8:28). We have seen how in John 17:18 we (as disciples) are brought into the Son's prayer to his Father: 'As You sent Me into the world, I also have sent them into the world.' We are commissioned into the world in just the same way as Jesus was. We cannot argue that Jesus was the Son of God and therefore a special case because he was living in communication with his Father all the time. Yet when we are sent into ministry we often act differently. We think we have not got time to pray, so we get others to do the praying while we do the 'ministry'. We get someone else to do the administration and so on. This will not do! We are sent to continue the same mission as Jesus in exactly the same way: that is, to remain in communication with the Father, doing what he does and saying what he says (John 5:19–20).

4. Jesus prayed from a pure heart

George Muller's favourite verse regarding prayer was 'If I regard wickedness in my heart, the Lord will not hear' (Psalm 66:18). Muller had success in prayer and in receiving answers, he maintained, because he kept his heart open, empty and clean before God. We cannot hope to misuse our hearts because they are not seen by the world and think that, somehow or other, God cannot see and will hear us when we pray. He might hear us, but we have no right to expect it. That is why we need clean hearts, why we need to keep 'short accounts' with God, and why we need to be in a place where the Lord continuously freshens us up and cleanses us, day by day (1 John 1:5–10).

5. Jesus encouraged us to pray together

The church must pray. In Matthew 18:19–20 Jesus tells us that 'if two of you agree on earth about anything that they may ask, it shall be done for them by My Father who is in heaven. For where two or three have gathered together in My name, I am there in their midst.' We are also told (verse 18) 'whatever you bind on earth shall have been bound in heaven'. There is power in corporate praying, in being in agreement. It is a power that is sometimes necessary if we are to get energy and strength enough to push the enemy out of a situation.

This requirement to pray together is not a contradiction of Jesus' instruction to us to 'go into your inner room, close your door and pray to your Father who is in secret, and your Father who sees what is done in secret will reward you' (Matthew 6:6). Sometimes we do not have the necessary strength and faith to find answers on our own. We need the power that comes through agreement.

We can see several instances of corporate prayer in Acts. In 1:14 '[The disciples] all with one mind were continually devoting themselves to prayer, along with the women, and Mary the mother of Jesus, and with His brothers.' In 2:42 'They were continually devoting themselves to the apostles' teaching and to fellowship, to the breaking of bread and to prayer.' Corporate prayer is extremely powerful, as we see in 4:23–31:

When [Peter and John] had been released, they went to their own companions and reported all that the chief priests and the elders had said to them. And when they heard this, they lifted their voices to God with one accord and said, 'O Lord, it is You who made the heaven and the earth and the sea, and all that is in them, who [spoke] by the Holy Spirit, through the mouth of our father David Your servant' ... And when they had prayed, the place where they had gathered together was shaken, and they were all filled with the Holy Spirit and began to speak the word of God with boldness.

The early church was continually praying together, taking seriously what the Lord had taught.

If we follow Christ's example in prayer we will find we have all the necessary resources for all that he wants us to do.

Paul-like prayer

In Ephesians there are two prayers of the Apostle Paul and an exhortation to us to pray. In all three places prayer and power are intimately connected. It seems that there is an order or theme within the text that progresses throughout the letter. The epistle falls into three sections: Paul gives us three chapters of doctrinal input (1 – 3); he then moves on to how this is expressed as we walk it out here on earth (4:1 – 6:9); he finally arrives at an encouragement to spiritual warfare (6:10–24). This threefold development of the six chapters of Ephesians is summed up by Watchman Nee as 'Sit' (1:20, 2:6), 'Walk' (4:1,17, 5:1–8,15) and 'Stand' (6:11,13–14). This progression through the whole epistle allows us to see a similar progression in the three passages that are concerned with prayer.

Paul's first prayer is particularly full of *thanksgiving* (1:16–23); the second is *worship* centred (3:14–21); and the third is a prayer of *intercession* (6:10–20). There is a progression in the text that reflects the mind of the Holy Spirit as the apostle moves from thanksgiving to worship to intercession.

It is interesting to note that one of the criticisms of spiritual warfare is that people claim worship is a weapon. The objection is that there is no place in the Bible that actually says that worship should be used as a weapon against the enemy. However, there is a verse that says, 'Yet You are holy, O You who inhabit the praises of Israel' (Psalm 22:3). 'To inhabit' means 'to be enthroned', which in turn means that the Lord reigns in the praises of his people. If the Lord is reigning he is getting his will done through worship, and his will is against evil. Very well, we do not have to use the word 'weapon', as the Bible does not, but if we do not first thank God, if we do not worship, we are not going to find very much power in the weapon of intercession. Worship lies behind intercession just as giving thanks lies behind worship. The more we thank and worship the more we will be able to intercede.

1. Read Ephesians 1:15–23

It is characteristic of Paul's letters that as he recalls his prayers for the Ephesians he pours them out again as he continues to write. He does not turn from prayer in his epistle until the beginning of chapter 2! We often get to hear Paul's prayers because he forgets about the epistle he is writing and records his intercession instead. Perhaps we should think about writing all of our letters out of a flow of prayer.

As Paul gives thanks and remembers before God all that the Ephesians have done, and their potential for the kingdom, he begins to recognise the power of God at work. Thus he goes on to speak about 'the surpassing greatness of His power toward us who believe' (1:19). But first he prays for the Ephesians to receive 'a spirit of wisdom and revelation in the knowledge of Him' (1:17). Similarly, as we pray, opening up to God in thanksgiving, we also open up our hearts to the Spirit of wisdom and revelation so that we might actually *see* the power that is coming out towards us. We need a vision of Jesus if we are to know what kind of inheritance is available to us. We need to be able to recognise the greatness of this power if we are to be able to take hold of it. We only appropriate what we first appreciate! This is why Paul prays for the Ephesians in this way – so that the glory of Jesus, the outshining of his greatness, might radiate towards them, and so that they might see who Jesus really is. Jesus is the resurrection! Jesus is enthroned (1:20)! He has his feet on the footstool of the earth! He, who is head over everything, is given to the church (1:22)!

This is the kind of power that is towards us. It is colossal. We will never come to the end of it. And yet we need to move from the power that comes towards us into the power that dwells within us.

2. Read Paul's second prayer in Ephesians 3:14–21

It is as we worship that the glory gets inside us; and as the glory gets inside us it changes into love. We receive this power as we worship, as we adore God and take him into our arms, hearts and lives. This, then, is why this prayer is a worshipping prayer, and talks about love.

Ephesians 1:19 spoke of the power towards us. Here it is the power that works within us (3:20). Why? What has happened? What has happened is that the thanksgiving has changed to worship and the glory has changed to love, and as we worship we receive God's power in us in the form of his love.

3. Read Ephesians 6:10–20, an exhortation to us to pray

In the context of giving the good news throughout the world today spiritual warfare is done by a praying church that puts on the armour and thrusts with the sword through all prayer and supplication. Prayer and supplication is the channel through which the power and the might of God are exerted into a situation. We give thanks to God, we worship God, then we direct the power of God into the specific area where it is needed. This is how the power is released from us and where our authority lies. This whole image of a soldier in armour is dependent on his feet. The soldier has got to stand to be effective (Ephesians 6:11,13,14). Yet the shoes on his feet are 'the preparation of the gospel'.

It is only an evangelising church that knows how to do 'spiritual warfare' properly. As we seek to win people for Christ we will find ourselves confronting the spiritual powers that hold them and we will be driven to prayer to see them released. 'He has sent me to proclaim release to the captives' (Luke 4:18).

A church that doesn't engage in evangelism, but mystically retreats from the world will not exert effective warfare.

3

The Lord's Prayer

What should we pray?

The Lord's Prayer must be the best-known prayer in the whole world. It is not long. I remember finding a farthing when I was a child, a tiny coin, smaller than a penny, and the whole of the Lord's Prayer was written on one side. This prayer, given by Jesus himself to teach us how to pray, must be the most 'prayed' prayer in the world. Yet many people do not really understand it, which is a great pity, because it is a wonderful prayer. There is no other like it.

Christians who believe in having a living, personal relationship with God, who encourage spontaneity in prayer and do not believe in 'institutions' or in being too formal, are sometimes rather suspicious when it comes to praying the Lord's Prayer because it could sound ritualistic. If, as sometimes happens, it is chanted mindlessly, recital does become akin to turning a 'prayer wheel', hoping that something will happen. But there are reasons why the Lord gave us this prayer.

The Lord's Prayer occurs in two slightly different contexts in the New Testament, in Matthew 6:9–13 and Luke

11:2–4. In Luke it is cited in response to the disciples' request: 'teach us how to pray'. It is vitally important for any discussion on prayer to take the Lord's Prayer into account because Jesus gave it as an answer to the same request that is in our hearts today. We need to be listening to what the Lord is saying to us so that we respond in prayer and begin to talk with him.

In Matthew, however, the Lord's Prayer is not cited in response to a request. Before commencing the Sermon on the Mount (Matthew 5 – 7) Jesus looks out on the multitudes. Matthew 5:1–2 say: 'When Jesus saw the crowds, He went up on the mountain; and after He sat down, His disciples came to Him. He opened His mouth and began to teach them, saying ...' Here, therefore, Jesus' teaching was in response to the need of the multitude – people who did not know God's truth and who looked for help; people who were in the darkness and the shadow of death. Jesus opened his mouth and began to teach them. He taught them many things – 'love your enemies' (Matthew 5:44), 'You are the salt of the earth' (Matthew 5:13) – and how to pray: 'Pray, then, in this way: "Our Father who is in heaven ..."' (6:9).

There are two good reasons for praying the Lord's Prayer as it is positioned in Matthew:

- Because of our relationship with God: we need to know how to talk to God. Human beings can do nothing so honouring and dignified as talking to God. It is the most fantastic thing that we have the privilege, right and honour of talking to our Creator.

- Because of our relationship with the world: there is nothing more important when we are talking to God than to look out to the multitude and say: 'How on earth can we reach them?' This is why the Lord taught the crowds and his disciples this prayer – because this is the way to reach those who do not know God. Praying is a part of Christian living and it is by Christian living that we are going to reach the multitudes.

We see in Matthew 4:23 onwards that Jesus went throughout Galilee healing, exorcising demons and blessing people. Large crowds followed him, and 'When Jesus saw the crowds, He went up on the mountain' (5:1). *We* look at the multitudes and say, 'I'd better go and lay hands on everybody, preach to them and give out tracts!' We wear ourselves out because there are so many people with so many needs. How will we reach them all? Jesus shows us that the way to get to the world is to come with him up on to the mountainside and listen to what he has to teach us.

If we were to start to live as Jesus teaches in Matthew 5, 6 and 7 the world would be evangelised overnight! Even though there are people who will not receive the gospel we would get the good news spreading through the world like wildfire! But because people see that we do not live by what we preach, they get 'turned off', and do not receive the good news.

If we were living as the Sermon on the Mount teaches, many people would be saved. People would want to know how to live like this. They would want to love and care for one another as the early Christians did, when it was said of them, 'See how they love one another!' This is the way in which Jesus wants the world to be reached.

Francis of Assisi (a medieval Christian and radical thinker) said, 'In everything that you do preach the good news of Jesus and, if necessary, use words!' We do also need to preach with words, but if we were living and being the good news as well as preaching the good news the world would soon be evangelised!

The Lord's Prayer appears nearly halfway through the Sermon on the Mount, which is right in the heart of Christian living. 'Whoever slaps you on your right cheek, turn the other to him also.' 'Whoever forces you to go one mile, go with him two.' 'Therefore you are to be perfect, as your heavenly Father is perfect.' 'Everyone who hears these words of Mine and acts on them, may be compared to a wise man who built his house on the rock.' 'Let your light shine before men in such a way that they may see your good works, and glorify your Father who is in heaven.'

How on earth are we going to live like this? If you go right to the heart of the Sermon on the Mount you are told how.

The Lord's Prayer is to teach us and enable us to live in the way that Jesus came to show us. There are some people who try to turn the other cheek, go the second mile, do good works, but without prayer they finish up having nervous breakdowns, because it is very difficult to live the Sermon on the Mount. Anyone who thinks that it is not has never really tried to live it! You cannot live any of the things that Jesus taught here unless you pray. Praying the Lord's Prayer brings you into a living relationship with God. Then not only do you know how to do these things, but you have the power to do them – power that, without prayer, you have not got!

Watchman Nee tells of two Chinese coolies who had a paddy field on top of a mountain. They had become Christians. Every night they pumped up water into a trough so that in the morning they could release the water and irrigate their field. One day they found that the trough had already been emptied and their water channelled down to the field below. All their hard work was wasted! 'Now,' they said to one another, 'we are Christians: what shall we do?'

They had been reading the Sermon on the Mount and the Lord had said, 'Give to him who asks.' Well, no one had actually asked, but they decided to do as Jesus said. They pumped the water up again, started late, finished late, came back next morning – and their water had gone again!

'What do we do now?' said one to the other.

'We are Christians – what does Jesus say?'

Jesus had said, 'Go the second mile,' so they decided that they would say nothing. Once more they started late, finished late, came back the next morning, and the water had gone again!

After some hard thought, one asked the other, 'What else did Jesus say?'

Jesus had said, 'Turn the other cheek!'

You will not be surprised to hear that these two new Christians were not particularly happy in repeating this task, but they themselves were very surprised to find that they were not happy. Jesus had also said, 'If you know these things, you are blessed if you do them' (John 13:17).

Something was wrong. So they resolved, 'If Jesus said this and it is not working, we need to find out why.'

They went to an older Christian and he said, 'What did Jesus tell you to do?'

'Well, give to him who asks, turn the other cheek, go the second mile ...'

'No', said the older Christian, 'did you not ask him what to do? Did you not pray?'

'Oh!' said our two new Christians. 'We have got to pray?!'

They went right to the heart of the Sermon on the Mount and prayed. One lifted up his head and said, 'I know what we have got to do! We have got to go and fill up the other fellows' trough first.'

The other man lifted up his head and said, 'Yes! Wonderful!'

And off they went. And they were very happy. As soon as the men in the field below had gone, they filled up their trough, then filled up their own, and went home. When they came back next morning their water was still there. They did the same thing the second day. The following morning the men from the field below came up and said, 'What is this Christianity – we want to know more!' They too were converted.

There may be a thousand and one ways of turning the other cheek in a Chinese paddy field. We all know what Jesus taught, but how do we apply his teaching to different situations? I do not really know, I have not got the power to know, and I am certainly not going to be happy doing it unless I talk to the Lord. That is why prayer is at the heart of the Sermon on the Mount. We cannot live the Christian

life without prayer – it won't work, because prayer is at the
very heart of it. Jesus did not come to give us a new list of
laws, a new Ten Commandments. He came to teach us to
pray! If we could not keep the Ten Commandments properly, how are we going to get anywhere with the Sermon
on the Mount, unless we learn how to pray?

Matthew 6:5 says: 'When you pray, you are not to be like
the hypocrites ...' The word 'hypocrite' is used thirteen times
in Matthew but only three times in Luke and once in Mark.
Matthew must have been particularly concerned about
hypocrites! The Greek word is *hupokritēs* and also means
'actor' – somebody playing a part. 'When you pray, you are
not to be like the "street actors"; for they love to stand and
pray in the synagogues and on the street corners so that they
may be seen.' Jesus does not mean that a person who prays
in the street is to be immediately labelled a hypocrite. He or
she might be, but it all depends on whether his or her
motive is 'to be seen by people'. If his or her motive is simply to look like a great pray-er, then the Lord would say that
he or she is a hypocrite! He is not interested in that kind of
thing. You may want to be a great pray-er, but this is not for
everyone else to know – it should be between you and
God. There are people who pray just because they think
others are listening. We have all been in prayer meetings
where people have prayed 'horizontally' – telling others
what they should be or do – particularly if there is someone
there who has upset them! It is fearful to pray like this and
those who do so had better be careful! It is insulting to the
Lord. Have you ever been with somebody who, when all
the time he or she is talking to you, is looking all around?

You feel like saying, 'Look at me when you're talking to me!' If we pretend that we are talking to God when we are really looking at someone else, we are being hypocrites! Jesus says, 'Truly I say to you, they [the hypocrites] have their reward in full' (Matthew 6:5). What is their 'full reward'? They wanted to be seen by people, and they were! But this kind of prayer is not going to enable them to live the Sermon on the Mount and therefore reach the multitude.

Matthew 6:6–7 read:

> But you, when you pray, go into your inner room, close your door and pray to your Father who is in secret, and your Father who sees what is done in secret will reward you. And when you are praying, do not use meaningless repetition as the Gentiles do, for they suppose that they will be heard for their many words.

In Palestinian houses at this time not many rooms had doors – one room just opened on from another. However, there was always one place where important papers and treasures were kept: a private cupboard. Jesus is saying, 'Go and shut yourself in the cupboard, close the door and pray to your Father in secret.' This is the place to pray: where nobody can see you. The Father, of course, is everywhere, but he particularly meets us in secret, and it is our privilege to meet with him one to one in this way, where there is intimacy and closeness.

If, as a father, I call my son and say, 'I want to talk to you' and he starts babbling, 'I didn't mean to do it, Dad! It just slipped out of my hand!' I know that he is feeling guilty! We do this in case our father has something to say to us. But our many words do not get our Father to listen to us. The word that Jesus uses in Matthew 6:7, 'Gentiles', means non-Jews – people who hadn't had the privilege of the Jewish people's history; who hadn't benefited from all the things that God had taught the Jews. People who do not know any better do believe that if they talk for long enough and use enough words they will induce God to listen to them. But this is not the way to pray. The Gentiles prayed like this because they thought that by their 'many words' they would get God's attention. But this can be gained by just a little cry – doesn't a baby get its mother's attention just by crying? We will get the Father's attention because he loves and cares for us and treats us as his daughters and sons.

A human father often wants to talk to his children more than they seem to want to speak to him. God is like this: he wants to hear us talk to him. As soon as we begin to speak he listens. A loving father does not have to be induced with multitudes of words. So do not pray with repetitions, many words and long ramblings: think carefully and pray precisely, knowing that the Father is listening. When we pray in secret we have no one to impress: 'So do not be like them; for your Father knows what you need before you ask Him' (Matthew 6:8). 'Even before there is a word on my tongue, behold, O Lord, You know it all,' says the Psalmist (Psalm 139:4). Before we are even expressing them, the Father knows our thoughts – but he still likes to hear them! It is possible to ask quietly without saying anything, but it is much easier to use words, and if you talk out loud you are making specific whatever you want to say to the Lord. This is a real conversation. 'Pray, then, in this way,' says Jesus (Matthew 6:9), and goes on to give us this model prayer.

Our Father who is in heaven,
Hallowed be Your name.
Your kingdom come.
Your will be done,
On earth as it is in heaven.
Give us this day our daily bread.
And forgive us our debts, as we also have forgiven our debtors.
And do not lead us into temptation,
but deliver us from evil.

Some later versions continue:

For Yours is the kingdom
and the power and the glory
forever. Amen.

We are not going to worry about these last few lines. The pure prayer as Jesus gave it to us ends at Matthew 6:13.

Did you notice that in the first two verses the prayer reads 'Hallowed be *Your* name', '*Your* kingdom come', '*Your* will be done', whereas in the last two or three verses this becomes 'Give *us*', 'forgive *us*', 'do not lead *us*', 'deliver *us*'? We are to begin by talking to the Lord about his interests. But do we? Most of us when we begin to pray say, 'Lord, I'm going to have a really rough day, I've got all this to do ...' But the Lord says, 'When you pray, start by talking about my things.' The Lord did not come to make us more selfish, rather capable of

thinking about other people and of his purpose on earth. Three
times 'your', then four times 'us'. Notice that it is not 'me' – it
is 'us'! This is because when we are alone with the Father, praying in our secret place, we are praying on behalf of everybody
else. The Lord is not keen for us to be self-centred and self-
indulgent when we pray, but we so very often are. This model
prayer reminds us that we are praying firstly for God's will and
secondly for other people – they are with us in this business of
living, and they should come into our prayers too! If we are to
be blessed we want them to be blessed also! If God answers our
prayers in a wonderful way we want others to be blessed too!
We are to pray 'us' prayers, not just 'me' prayers.

Three ways in which to understand and pray the Lord's Prayer

1. Eschatologically

There is a very real sense in which the Lord's Prayer is looking towards God's will being done on earth. Therefore,
when we pray we must look forward to God's kingdom
coming. There are lots of kingdoms around in the world,
but it is only his kingdom that we want! We must look forward to the day when God will reign and bring righteousness to the whole earth. This is one way of understanding
the Lord's Prayer: it is a prayer for the kingdom of Jesus'
return; a prayer for the future when, unlike now, everything
done on earth will be in accordance with God's perfect will.
It is a prayer for daily bread, or as a closer translation reads,

for the 'bread of tomorrow' – the banquet bread of the future marriage supper of the Lamb tasted before time! 'Forgiveness' is the final verdict of God on our earthly lives, while 'temptation' is understood as the trial by which the evil one, our accuser, will try to resist our entry into glory, so we ask to be delivered from him.

2. Ecclesiastically

Ecclesiastically means 'relating to the church'. Just as we can pray the Lord's Prayer eschatologically we can also apply the prayer to 'where we are at the moment' and to what is happening in the church now until the day Christ returns. God is our Father now and his name is to be 'hallowed' or 'made holy' by his children (Isaiah 8:13, 29:22–23). God acts in the present in power to bring salvation, healing and deliverance, the evidence of his kingdom on earth. Indeed, some early church fathers and two late New Testament manuscripts substitute 'Holy Spirit come upon us and cleanse us' for 'Your kingdom come'. This is not wrong, as an interpretation for the Kingdom of God is 'righteousness, peace and joy *in the Holy Spirit*' (Romans 14:17). God also provides for the daily needs of his children in the present life.

3. Emotionally

Emotionally, many things inside us militate against prayer. The Lord's Prayer will deal with those emotions that would stop us praying, if we treat it properly. Guilt, fear and a low sense of self-worth stop us praying – 'I'm too bad to pray!' 'What if God is angry with me?' 'God never hears my prayers anyway!' And so on. If we use it as Jesus intended the Lord's Prayer will heal us so that we can really pray.

Let us think about the emotional aspect of the prayer, taking it phrase by phrase.

'Our Father who is in heaven,
Hallowed be Your name.'

When we use the word 'Father' in our prayer we have to see ourselves as sons and daughters of God, not as less than that. We are not just mere human beings, we are not even sinful human beings (even though we are both sinful and human) – we are sons and daughters of God! We are coming to our Father! This is family business.

The majority of people, because of sin, because of the way they have been put down in life, and because of people who have trampled all over them (sometimes, sadly, their own fathers and mothers) do not see themselves as being part of the family of God. When we are born again God brings us into a place where we can say 'Father' (Romans 8:15) and we come into a family. That family is a place of healing – a place where we find acceptance, where people love us and care for us and say we are worth something. The family of God should be a place where others by their body language and by the way they look at us say, 'You are accepted, you are loved, you are welcome, for this is the family of God and God is our Father!' All of our insecurity begins to soak away in the Father's presence, and when that happens we begin to pray properly. We find our faith in him growing ever deeper. We have got to pray with faith, not because our faith is marvellous, but because the Father is marvellous! Here is the beginning of receiving healing in our lives.

One night a Christian friend of mine had a great experience of the Holy Spirit. Afterwards, he praised the Lord, and then tried to go to sleep. But he heard a voice saying, 'Allah!' 'Allah!' By now it was about two o'clock in the morning. My friend thought, 'That's strange! Here am I worshipping Jesus and I keep hearing "Allah, Allah!"' He rightly thought that perhaps he should go and look at the Qur'an he had kept from his travelling days. Now, there are ninety-nine references to Jesus in the Qur'an; there are Muslims today finding Jesus in its pages. My friend read in the Qur'an about the virgin birth of Jesus, the fact that he was perfect, performed miracles, and did not sin. He read that Jesus went back to God and is coming again – all these things are there. Afterwards he read his Bible until it was time to go off to the local technical college to a meeting of the Christian Union, where he was due to speak.

When he arrived, the Christian Union president was looking terribly distraught. He told my friend that he had had some trouble with four Muslim students from the Middle East. 'They came to the meeting last week,' he said. 'They were shouting out questions and wouldn't be quiet and the meeting ended in chaos. And they've come again today!'

The meeting started, and as my friend began to speak one of the students shouted out, 'You say that nobody can come to God except by Jesus Christ!'

My friend quietly prayed and then said, 'Oh no, we do not say that. Jesus said, "No man comes to the *Father* except through me." You might know God as Creator; you might know him as Judge; but you do not know him as a Father, do you? You have many names for God, but not one of them is Father, is it? If you would only call Jesus "Son of God" you would find the Father. Then you too could call God "Father".'

My friend continued, but the next student shouted something out. 'Excuse me,' said my friend, 'have you been reading the New Testament? Where did you get these questions from?'

The student was very honest. 'Oh no, I have a book here called *Difficult Questions To Ask Christians!*'

My friend was a little taken aback! But he said quietly, 'I read the Qur'an this morning for two hours. I suggest that you go and read the New Testament and then come back and ask these questions.'

The students didn't say another word for the rest of the meeting! One fellow did come back six weeks later. He gave his life to Jesus.

To know God as Father we must come to the Son knowing that he has died for us and that he loves us. He can then open up our hearts, for 'no one comes to the Father but through Me' (John 14:6). 'Nor does anyone know the Father except the Son, and anyone to whom the Son wills to reveal Him' (Matthew 11:27). 'Come to Me, all who are weary and heavy-laden, and I will give you rest' (Matthew 11:28). We learn to pray with our hearts freed from the sense of 'no worth' because God has said 'You are my child.'

The Lord knows each one of us individually and as a Father he hears our prayers. Even though there are billions of other prayers he knows your prayers specifically and treats each one of us equally.

> 'Your kingdom come.
> Your will be done,
> On earth as it is in heaven.'

The trouble with most of us is that we cannot get our own will done. Thus we get frustrated and angry. In any case, to get our will done is, in the end, virtually impossible. But if we give our wills to God, to help him get his will done on earth, then we will see something happen – we'll see his kingdom come!

Jesus said, 'if I cast out demons by the Spirit of God, then the kingdom of God has come upon you' (Matthew 12:28). Getting God's kingdom to 'come upon us', getting his will done 'on earth as it is in heaven' – this is success. Success is getting things done God's way in God's world: bringing 'righteousness and peace and joy in the Holy Spirit' on earth as it is in heaven (Romans 14:17).

People think that if they have a lot of money they will be able to do what they like. In a sense they can! But it won't release a lot of justice, joy and peace. They will still get frustrated and they will still get angry. There is only one way to solve frustration and anger, and that is to say, 'Lord, we want your will to be done.' As C.S. Lewis wrote in *The Great Divorce* there are, in the end, only two kinds of people: those who say to God 'Thy will be done' and those to whom God says 'Thy will be done.' Praying that his will be done removes the frustration that destroys prayer.

'Give us this day our daily bread.'

We are to pray for our needs and not worry about them. Worry and anxiety kill prayer, because instead of praying we are thinking, 'What if I don't get my daily bread?' If you are constantly careworn, remember that you must 'ask in faith without any doubting, for the one who doubts is like the surf of the sea, driven and tossed by the wind ... that man ought not to expect that he will receive anything from the Lord' (James 1:6–8). Our prayer life is hindered when we are worried about ordinary, everyday earthly things. The Lord wants us to be in a place where anxiety and worry disappear, so that we can pray properly. Those who worry even when they have nothing to worry about need to get into God's presence, to clear the decks, and say: 'What on earth am I worrying about? "Why should I charge my soul with care? The wealth in every mine belongs to Christ, God's son and heir. Yes, he is a friend of mine, and he with me does all things share."' When we cease to worry, then we pray properly, and then we can receive answers to our prayer.

'And forgive us our debts'

Our debts are the things that we owe God, but sometimes things that we owe other people too. When David says (in Psalm 51:4) 'Against You, You only, I have sinned' I think this is stretching it a little. Of course, all sin is ultimately against

God, but David had taken Uriah's wife and then put Uriah in the front line of battle so that he was killed (see 2 Samuel 11). And then he says to God 'Against You, You only, I have sinned'!

We do sin against each other and we do owe a debt to one another for the things we do wrong. But God, behind it all, does not want us to be doing all these wrongs – it grieves his heart. And so Jesus tells us to pray 'forgive us our debts' – our sins. Some people get upset when we keep praying for our sins to be forgiven: they complain that we are 'miserable sinners' and so on. Perhaps we should say that we are happy sinners! Since we do sin (and there is no point in pretending that we do not) it is far better to be overly sensitive about it, because sin is very, very serious. But God wants us to bring our sins to him and to make sure that they are forgiven so that there is true happiness.

Having a 'short account' with God is important. It means taking to the Lord the things that he shows you in your heart, the things that you have done wrong that day, and so getting them out of the way. It is important because the Father wants to keep us happy. Even though as Christians we may know that our sins have been forgiven, that we will not have to pay God's final penalty of execution, we still need to receive continual, daily forgiveness from the Father so that we feel in healthy and close relationship with him. Unforgiven sin gets in the way of relationship because guilt, anger and hurt create a barrier between the two parties.

Asking for forgiveness is not always a matter of ultimate guilt and capital punishment, of deserving to be taken out and executed. That was dealt with as Jesus hung on the cross. However, we should ask forgiveness for the

day-to-day things where we fall out of line with God and
with each other. We owe it to God (and to one another) to
pray 'Forgive us our debts as we forgive our debtors', for
then the Lord will cleanse us and the guilt will go. Guilt is
a killer to our prayer life. If we feel guilty we do not pray.
We think: 'God is not going to listen to me.' Sometimes
when we sin very badly not only do we not pray, we do not
even go to meetings. We punish ourselves, hoping that God
will feel sorry for us. But Hebrews 10:26 warns us that there
are no more sacrifices for sin, not even self-sacrifice. Only
Jesus' sacrifice can deal with sin, so there is only one way to
be rid of sin: 'If we confess our sins, He is faithful and righteous to forgive us our sins and to cleanse us from all
unrighteousness' (1 John 1:9). Tell Father about it: the guilt
goes and we are able to begin to believe that our prayers
will be answered again after all.

'As we also have forgiven our debtors.'

If, when we pray, we are bitter and twisted about the way
that people have treated us; if we feel hurt and know that
we are not forgiving someone, that will also spoil our prayer
life. Bitterness kills prayer.

A lady who had been very badly treated by two different
men and who as a consequence had become extremely hard
and bitter had a daughter who was converted and started to
come along to meetings. Sometimes her mother would
come to the meeting to collect her. The first time I ever
spoke to her, she said to me, 'You're not going to get me
converted!'

I said to her, 'Be careful, because people like you who say that sort of thing get converted before they know where they are!'

Fortunately, she had a good sense of humour, and she laughed and took her daughter home. The funny thing was that the next Sunday she was there with her daughter. I was preaching that evening and after the meeting she said to me, 'That book talks, doesn't it!'

'Yes,' I said, 'and it makes a lot of sense.' Just by chance I happened to have a copy of John's Gospel in my pocket, so I offered it to her, saying, 'Why don't you take this home and read it?'

The next week she came again and said, 'I want to be a Christian.'

We prayed together, and she accepted Jesus, but she still felt bound up and bitter because of all the wrongs that had been done to her. She prayed again on Monday but nothing changed, and on Tuesday, but still she felt no freer. On Wednesday she prayed and said, 'Lord, it's no good, I can never be a Christian because I cannot forgive.' And even as she confessed her inability to forgive to the Lord she knew she was forgiven and she knew that she could forgive!

You have to take the ground of forgiveness – even if you do not feel like it – and know that it is right, for then God can meet you. It is ridiculous to go to God saying, 'Please forgive me,' and then say, 'But I'm not going to forgive such and such' – this is approaching on the wrong ground! God can only forgive on the ground of forgiveness. We take that ground by talking to God. We can tell him, 'I can't do it Lord,' and he replies, 'That's alright, because I can!' We can receive his forgiveness when we are willing to forgive others. Unwillingness to forgive hinders and harms our lives so that we do not pray properly.

The Lord's Prayer helps us to understand the importance of our forgiving others if we are to expect forgiveness for ourselves. There are many other things that need prayer. How will I pay the gas bill? Will I get a job? We need to talk about these things, but to get into the right place to start talking we have to clear unforgiveness out of the way!

'And do not lead us into temptation, but deliver us from evil.'

Lots of people think that it is a bit odd to say 'lead us not into temptation', but this is the Aramaic way of putting it – Aramaic language (the language that Jesus spoke) is constructed differently from ours. It simply means: 'Do not let me get into situations where I might be tempted.' It does not mean that the Lord might actually guide us into temptation (although this is what it looks like in English), but that he will 'deliver us from the evil one', out of the hands of the devil. It is from the devil, from the fear of temptation, from the fear of falling and from the fear of failing that we ask the Lord to deliver us.

Many people say to me, 'I can't become a Christian, I would never be able to keep it up.' This fear can keep us from God altogether. Many people are kept in bondage by fear, particularly the fear of death. Sometimes the devil keeps people in fear of death throughout their whole lifetime. Jesus came to abolish death and the fear of it. Fear will hinder both our prayer and our faith that God is hearing us. Fear will prevent us from receiving from the Lord. When we pray the Lord's Prayer we are praying in the groundwork so that we can bring all our requests to him with thanksgiving and actually start to receive from him.

These above assertions of the Lord's Prayer get rid of all the basic human emotional problems that bruise, hurt and hinder us in our faith. If we come to Jesus praying this prayer on the grounds that he taught us to pray it, then he must want to respond to it – and he will!

What more should we pray?

In Luke's Gospel the Lord's Prayer is given in shortened form (Luke 11:2–4). Jesus prayed and as the disciples watched they longed to be able to commune with the Father as he was doing (11:1). Consequently, they asked him, 'Lord, teach us to pray.' It was because Jesus prayed that the disciples wanted to pray. People do not pray when they are told to pray. They cannot be made to pray. People pray when they see others pray. If leaders are seen to be prayerful then everyone else will start to pray too. Luke here shows the disciples' response to Jesus' prayer life.

Prayer must be important to us and at the heart of who we are as disciples if we truly are people who are learning to have a meaningful and powerful relationship with Jesus. If we do not pray we will not realise that relationship. When we do pray we will find that it is not always easy work, and as we try to make it easier it gets harder and harder. But praying is to be at the heart of our Christian lives, so we too must ask, 'Lord, teach us to pray!'

We are now going to look at the context in which the Lord's Prayer appears in Luke.

The Lord's Prayer 'contextually'

In Luke 10:38–42, just prior to the Lord's Prayer, we find the story of Martha and Mary. Mary is sitting at the Lord's feet, listening to what he is saying. This is the beginning of understanding how to pray. When God speaks to us we want to speak back. If we start talking to the Lord without listening first we often dry up before long. But if we listen to the Lord talking, as Mary did, we can talk back to him in response. Obviously, different people use different patterns and methods when they pray, and one cannot say that it is a particular command of the Lord to do it this way. But some of us would probably do well to try it, just the same.

George Muller was a great pray-er. In the second half of the nineteenth century he kept two thousand orphaned children alive on 'air and prayer', never asking for financial support from others. George Muller knew how to pray when those children had nothing to eat. His method was simply to say every morning, 'Lord, please speak to me and teach me from your word.' Then he would read the Scriptures. When he had listened to God's word he would begin to bring all the problems, the difficulties and the challenges, together with the bills that were going to arrive that morning, to the Lord. Here is a man of prayer! George Muller was very much blessed in answer to prayer as he listened to the word of the Lord.

Mary also listened to the Lord. In Luke 11:1–13 we discover the importance of talking to the Lord in prayer. But only when we have let God's word come to us can we begin to speak our words back to him. Asking comes after listening to what the Lord is saying to us. And when we ask, we will receive the Holy Spirit – God's provision for all our needs. The way we release other people into communicating with God is by releasing the Spirit through our words. So when we have listened to God's word (like Mary), and when we have talked to God ourselves in prayer, we can go out and speak his word into other people's lives. That word will deliver them, set them free, and enable them to speak out and give glory to God. After explaining the Lord's Prayer, Jesus went on to release a mute man from the demon that was afflicting him (Luke 11:14–16). In the power of his prayer life, he let loose the activity of the Holy Spirit into the world around him.

Often people come up to me at the end of a meeting and say, 'Thank you for saying this or that, it really spoke to me.' When they tell me what I said I don't recognise it at all! In fact, I know that I did not say it, because I know it is not quite my style! What has really happened is that the Holy Spirit has been speaking, and what they heard was not something I said, but something the Spirit was saying in their hearts. It is the Lord who speaks to us; it is the Lord who releases people. If I am going to say anything or let someone hear something that is going to help I have to be listening to God to hear what he is saying.

Moreover, Luke 11:27–28 tells us that:

> While Jesus was saying these things, one of the women in the crowd raised her voice and said to Him, 'Blessed is the womb that bore You and the breasts at which You nursed.' But He said, 'On the contrary, blessed are those who hear the word of God and observe it.'

According to Jesus, a greater thing than giving birth to the Messiah is to hear the word of God and to do it! So, to sum up:

1. We listen to God's *word*

Luke 10:38–42
Mary and Martha

2. We talk with him about it and receive the *Spirit*

Luke 11:1–13
The Lord's Prayer

3. We go out and speak it and release the activity of the Holy *Spirit* into somebody else's life

Luke 11:14–26
Delivering the Mute Man

4. Having done all this, we come back to hear God's *word* again and do it!

Luke 11:27–28
Woman in the Crowd

The most wonderful and most important thing in our lives
is not only to listen to God, it is not only to talk to God, it
is not only to release other people in the name of God, it is
to do the word of God. There are people who do everything
else but who do not *obey* the word of God. If only it were
not like this! If only it were the people who know their
Bible backwards, who pray great prayers and talk to the Lord
a lot, who see wonderful manifestations or phenomena take
place – if only these were the people that God is most
pleased with. That would make it much easier to know who
the spiritual 'giants' really are. Unfortunately, in the final
analysis, it is to hear God's word and to do it that is most
important: to love your neighbour; to turn the other cheek;
to speak well of people who revile you; to pray when you
are put down; and to love your enemy (Luke 6:27–31). It is
those who hear God's word and put it into practice, those
who build their house on a rock and who when the rains
come find nothing shakes it (Luke 6:48) who show true spiritual majesty. The trouble is that the only person who knows
that you are doing the word of God (inwardly as well as outwardly) is the Lord himself! There is never any place for
boasting. If we do things for praise – fasting, giving alms and
praying – then we will have had our reward here on earth.
In the end, the truth of whether or not we are obedient to
the word of God is something that only God knows.

In 2 Corinthians 5:10 we are reminded that we all have to
stand before the judgement seat of Christ, and I, for one,
would like to be able to feel good about standing there. But
we are not all going to feel good about it, and I am
concerned sometimes that I will be one who does not. A holy

reverence and a proper fear of the Lord is the beginning of wisdom (Proverbs 9:10) and the day will come when we will have to stand before him. Only those who hear the word of God and do it, inside and outside of their lives, will be able to feel good about it. Just as Jesus, God's word, was conceived and brought forth by the Holy Spirit through Mary, so we must let the Spirit bring forth God's word through us.

The Lord's Prayer 'comparatively'

We have seen the Lord's Prayer in the context of Matthew and the context of Luke. Now let's look at the two versions of the prayer 'comparatively', in order to demonstrate its basic structure and the essence of its meaning. When Matthew's and Luke's versions are put alongside each other we can see six basic elements emerging. Luke's short version captures the essence of Matthew's longer version.

1. In Matthew we begin 'Our Father who is in heaven'. In Luke we just say 'Father', the word with which we approach God: 'Abba', 'Father'. The evidence that we are genuine sons and daughters of God is that we say 'Abba'. It spontaneously arises in our hearts to address God, not as the majestic, sovereign, eternal and immutable God-who-exists-in-eternity, but as 'Daddy'. Muslims never address God as 'Father' and Jews only talk about him as the 'Father of the Nation' in the light of the Old Testament. But Christians can come to him personally and say 'my Abba', for we have a personal, intimate relationship with God.

2. 'Hallowed be Your name' is not too meaningful in modern English. 'Hallowed' is just another way of saying 'Let it be holy', 'Let it be sanctified', but this is not easy to understand either! Isn't God's name holy already? One simple way of putting it is to say, 'Keep the family name in good standing.' This reminds us that we are his children and that we do not want to let his name down. Think of your own family name: there are people who carry your name who have done things that you do not like to be associated with. Others' actions have made you

	Matthew	Luke
1	Our Father *who is in Heaven*	Father
2	Hallowed be Your name	hallowed be Your name
3	Your Kingdom come, *Your will be done, on earth as it is in heaven*	your kingdom come
4	Give us this day our daily bread	Give us each day our daily bread
5	And forgive us our debts, as we also have forgiven our debtors	And forgive us our sins, for we ourselves also forgive everyone who is indebted to us
6	And do not lead us into temptation, *but deliver us from evil*	And lead us not into temptation

proud to bear it. Similarly, when it comes to the family of God, it is the way that we behave, what we do, and the way that we show respect for our Father that sanctifies (hallows, makes holy) the family name. As children of God the way that we live in the world either sanctifies the Father's name or it does not.[1]

3. In a sense, the extra sentence in Matthew's version – 'Your will be done, on earth as it is in heaven' – does not seem necessary. For the kingdom to come is the same thing as for God's will to be done. God's kingdom coming means God reigning – God getting his will done! How does our queen reign in this country? How does she get her will done? An earthly queen needs armies, navies and a police force – people who represent her. Through all these different channels she 'gets her will done in the United Kingdom as she does in Buckingham Palace'. She delegates the responsibility for carrying out her commands to the Prime Minister, the chief constable, or to the judges in the law courts, and they in turn see that her wishes are carried out. God works in the same way in his kingdom as the queen does in the United Kingdom. But just because God reigns in the kingdom of God does not mean that everything happens on earth exactly as he wants any more than that everything that happens in Britain is exactly what the queen wants! But she gets her will done and brings the country into order by using the bodies at her disposal. We are the body of Christ. We are not the kingdom – we are the body. It is through the body, the church, that God

gets his will done on earth. We do not talk about the church as 'the kingdom' because, as we are the sons and daughters of God, we are the family – the king's family. We are not the kingdom.

When we pray 'Your Kingdom come' we are asking that God's activity and the power of his Holy Spirit be released through the church into the world so that the world might know that God is reigning. If the church is sleeping, if it never calls on the Lord, if we do not pray, if we are simply looking after our own little kingdoms and doing our own thing, is it surprising that some people say, 'Well, I don't think that God is around at all – he doesn't seem to be doing very much!'? God does not seem to do much because he has committed himself to working through his body to reign in this world. He has committed himself to function together with his people, just as we are committed to function by using our bodies. We exert our power by using our bodies and in the same way God exerts his power on earth through the church. The church, therefore, cannot sleep, it cannot laze around – it has got to be available so that God can get his will done 'on earth as it is in heaven'.

This is a wonderful prayer. We can pray the shortened version (as in Luke) or the longer version from Matthew: they are equally good because they are saying the same thing!

4. The Lord wants us to pray this prayer in order that our earthly needs are met. Of course, it does not mean

---

[1] When God answers prayer in wondrous ways his name is sanctified as in Ezekiel 36:23.

that we only need bread, but all of our daily require-
ments.

5. Matthew says forgive us our 'debts'; Luke uses 'sins'.
Debts are things that we owe God and each other. A sin
is a disobedience to God, when we fail to give him what
we owe him. We owe it to God to live in his world his
way: otherwise we will mess it up. Sin entered because
we did not live his way: we disobeyed him. We owe it to
God to fulfil the purpose of our creation, for if we do
not, we have stolen our lives from him.

'As we forgive others' does not mean that God forgives us on the ground that we are willing to forgive
somebody else. The ground on which God forgives us is
the ground of the cross. It is the blood of Jesus that pays
the debt we owe. We are forgiven for Jesus' sake.
However, if we are to receive forgiveness we must be
willing to believe in forgiveness and so be in a place
where we are prepared to forgive others – we must forgive our debtors. We would be hypocrites if we were to
pray, 'Oh Lord, please forgive us – but we're not going to
forgive them!' If we are not prepared to forgive, we will
never know that we are forgiven! When we come to
God and say, 'I cannot forgive but I know that I ought to
– Lord help me!' God forgives us and we know that we
can forgive and will know forgiveness. We cannot receive
forgiveness if we do not repent of our hatred of others!
We have to change our ground. However, our forgiving
others is not the reason God forgives us – our being able
to receive forgiveness depends on our willingness to

forgive. Jesus further elucidates forgiveness in Matthew 18:21–35, where a forgiven man does not forgive and loses his spiritual freedom, being cast into prison. The church is the family of the forgiven and the forgiving.

6. We need to pray 'do not lead us into temptation' (which is just an Aramaic way of saying 'don't let it get into us!') because we are surrounded by temptation all the time. This does not mean that God puts temptation before us in order to test us, but that we are asking him to protect us from temptation and to keep us out of the hands of the devil – the evil one.

When we give into temptation we are opening the door to the enemy. That is why Matthew goes on to add 'deliver us from evil' (or 'the evil one'). I want to emphasise 'the evil one'. Jesus was able to say 'the ruler of the world [evil one] is coming, and he has nothing in Me' (John 14:30); but when the evil one comes to us he has got something in us, for when we sin we give him ground. Where we have given way to temptation, the devil sees it, and says, 'This is mine!' We may think that he has only a little hold on us, but it is not necessary to take hold of the whole of a body to take it prisoner: you need only put a manacle around a wrist! In Ephesians 4:27 Paul warns about giving ground (or room) to the enemy by giving into temptation. Once that ground belongs to the enemy he can shake us and we become more conscious of belonging to the enemy than we are of belonging to God. We belong to God, he has paid for us, but we have made room for the devil to put his hand in and shake us. So, Lord, 'Lead us not into temptation, but deliver us from the evil one.' In essence, Luke is saying the same as Matthew.

Jesus praying his own prayer

When his disciples asked Jesus to teach them to pray he did not just pluck some catchy phrases out of thin air and throw them together as an example for them. He used words and sentiments that he himself knew the good of praying in his daily life.

'Our Father who is in heaven, Hallowed be Your name.' When Jesus said this he knew what it was to pray to his Father. Every time Jesus prayed he always addressed God as 'Father': only once did he say, 'My God, My God', and this was on the cross, where he was experiencing everything a hell-condemned man would experience (Psalm 22). It is extraordinary, thrilling and fulfilling to think that God has become a man and has experienced everything that it means to be rejected by God. But everywhere else in his experience here on earth Jesus addresses God as 'Father'. In John 17 he says, 'Father, keep them in Your name, the name which You have given Me, that they may be one even as We are. While I was with them, I was keeping them in Your name.' He says to Thomas, 'If you had known Me, you would have known My Father also' (John 14:7). He was so in tune with his Father that he was always doing and saying what his Father was doing and saying. How could he have done this if he had not always remained in communion with his Father? How can we show what God is like in our lives unless we are saying, 'Father who is in heaven sanctified be your name'? Jesus had to pray *and live* his prayer – and he did it perfectly.

When we pray this prayer God will begin to show himself through us, albeit, because of our sin, imperfectly. But he will show himself through us. Imagine Jesus in the carpenter's shop at, say, seven years of age. He picks up a chisel and starts to chisel inexpertly. You can imagine Joseph saying, 'Hey! Stop it, son! Now, whenever you start to chisel, do it like this! Whenever you use a chisel always move it away from yourself – never bring it in, or you might do yourself some damage. Now watch me do it.' And Joseph would pick up the tool and chisel away and Jesus would copy him. This picture of Jesus in the carpenter's shop reflects our life when we reveal the Father to the world. We may copy imperfectly at times; we may make a mistake and cut ourselves, as the young Jesus was sure to have done. But as he followed his earthly father more and more closely he learned how to be a skilled carpenter. If we do not pray 'Our Father' how can we get anywhere near to what even Jesus knew he had to do, that is, to keep his eyes on his Father all the time? Jesus had to pray 'Your will be done, on earth as it is in heaven' more than once – in the Garden of Gethsemane he said, 'Father, if You are willing, remove this cup from Me; yet not My will, but Yours be done' (Luke 22:42). That is, 'Your kingdom come! I want you to reign in this situation!' And God did reign – he reigned over the enemies of Jesus, he reigned over Pontius Pilate, he reigned over those who played dice for his clothes, and he reigned over those who shouted, 'Save yourself and come down!' These things were in fulfilment of Psalm 22. God's will was being done on the cross, but Jesus realised that for God to be King the cost would be great. It would cost so much that he prayed (Luke 22:42) 'if You are willing, remove this cup from Me'. In those moments the Son of God had to accept the Father's will. His own will had to come second, his own will had to fit in with the Father's will; and in those moments he experienced the full cost of obedience. He learned obedience through the things that he suffered. Many of us have prayed asking that 'this cup should pass'. We may even have offered God alternatives as to how the problem could be solved! But it is when we start to say 'Not my will but yours be done' that we are truly in the place of a son. Jesus had 'King' written over him when he was on the cross. The early church fathers said 'He reigns from the tree' – thus he will reign from our crosses in life if we pray 'Your Kingdom come, your will be done.'

A first-century Jewish father could demand anything of his son: complete, total and utter obedience. The other side of the coin was this: the son would expect complete, total and utter commitment of the father to him. This is what Jesus was doing in Gethsemane. This is why Jesus rose again by the power of God – because his Father was committed to him. When it is hurtful and difficult and hard for us to say 'Your will be done' the Spirit of God will whisper in your ear 'Father is as committed to Son as Son is being asked to be committed to Father.' This is good news.

We need our daily bread, for 'man does not live by bread alone, but ... by everything that proceeds out of the mouth of the Lord' (Deuteronomy 8:3). When we pray 'Give us this day our daily bread' we are not just praying for earthly food, we are also praying for our spiritual daily bread. Jesus, too, lived on spiritual bread. In John 4:32–34 he says, 'I have food to eat that you do not know about ... My food is to do the will of Him who sent Me.' It is prayer that strengthens and sustains us. It is prayer that enables us to eat and to do the will of God. If we do not pray we become weak and flabby, when we do pray we become strong! As Jesus and his disciples went from village to village to bring the good news he rose early in the morning to go up into the mountains to pray – to receive his 'daily bread', his 'manna', and to find out his Father's will for the day. Isaiah 50:4 shows the Messiah receiving words for weary men and women, his daily work!

'And forgive us our sins, for we ourselves also forgive everyone who is indebted to us.' We might wonder, 'Why does Jesus need to pray for forgiveness?' Psalm 69 (which is called a 'messianic' psalm because it explicitly speaks of Jesus dying for us on the cross) calls the sins that the Messiah was carrying '*his* sins'. Do not be shocked by this: we know that they were our sins, but whilst Christ was on the cross the psalmist calls them 'his sins' because 'God's righteousness' is now our righteousness too! It is shocking, but it is true. The sins that Jesus died for (our sins) were so laid upon him that they were possessed by him and he experienced all the effects of these sins, just as the righteousness that he had (which he gave to us) is possessed by us! So Jesus also knows what it is to say 'forgive us our sins' and he also knows how to pray for 'everyone who is indebted to us'. If Jesus had not forgiven the sins of the people he met in his daily life he could not have said, when he came to the cross, 'Forgive, as I have forgiven those who have sinned against me.' But he did forgive, all the way through his life.

There is nothing more marvellous than the cross of our Lord Jesus Christ and he who hangs on that cross – the one who, right the way through his earthly life, was always forgiving. Therefore, when he came to the cross, he could justly pray 'Forgive us our sins as I have forgiven those who have sinned against me' because he was perfect and holy. From the cross Jesus calls upon his Father to deliver him from the effects of the outworking of sin, judgement and death until he rises again.

When did Jesus need delivering? Picture him in the grave. That body never did anything wrong! It always did the will of the Father; it was always loving, always true, always kind, gentle and forgiving. How could we think that God would leave that body there? These qualities will last forever: these are the eternal things, the things that belong to immortality. Of course the Father will raise them out of the grave! The resurrection has to be! God is committed to these things – they are what he is! Now they are found in a man, he must rise again! This is the man who prayed 'Do not lead me into the trial, into temptation, but O, Father deliver me from the evil one' – and the Father did! He was delivered out of the hands of Satan, sin and death.

The Lord's Prayer truly was Jesus' own prayer, inspired by a life that knew the necessity of constant communion with his Father.

4

Prophetic Prayer

'Prophetic prayer' is a term that is often bandied about. It belongs to the same category of terminology as, for instance, 'spiritual warfare' and 'territorial spirits'. Such vocabulary is, I think, gradually becoming 'honed down' into a more definitive way of understanding, but still there is often some confusion as to exactly what these terms mean. This kind of new terminology arises when the church is alive and well. Words like 'trinity' are not biblical but have come out of the theological enquiry and spiritual sensitivity of those trying to understand the prophetic Scriptures. We must understand the prophetic Scriptures by the Holy Spirit, who caused them to be written in the first place!

The Holy Spirit leads us into the truth of God's word and into the regions that are necessary at different times in church history. If there is anything that God is emphasising at this time I think that I can say without fear of contradiction that it is prayer, intercession and learning how to deal with the supernatural in the negative so that we can see more of it in the positive. This is the area that God is awaking within us in order that we might reach out into the final phases of world evangelisation. If we do not deal with these supernatural strongholds, establishments and powers throughout the earth, we are not going to see the work of world evangelism completed. But how do we move them? In essence, by prayer, but by prayer in the widest possible context.

The Spirit of God has gradually been leading us towards this area of prophetic prayer. Prophetic prayer comes from the prophetic church – not a church where one or two have a gift of prophecy, but a whole church that is becoming prophetic, and which engages in a dimension best described by the word 'prophetic'. When we begin to look into this, enquiring of God what it means to be a prophetic people – a people who are praying that we will have prophetic prayer – I feel that there is no better word that could be used. It is something that is bigger than just one or two words offered to God. It is something that must involve our whole calling as the people of God, if we are going to shift the spiritual powers that are opposed to us and go right through into fulfilling God's purpose for us.

The heart of God

Obviously, prophetic prayer is prayer related to prophecy. The whole church of our Lord Jesus Christ today is seen to be potentially prophetic. In the days of Moses the Spirit came upon the seventy elders as they were gathered together – but two were missing, Eldad and Medad (Numbers 11). However, they did not miss the blessing, for the Holy Spirit came upon them nonetheless! Joshua was very concerned that these two men were being blessed when they had not been present at the meeting – and we all know that isn't acceptable! – and rushed to tell Moses, whose response was very instructive. He said (prophetically), 'Would that all the Lord's people were prophets ...!' (Numbers 11:29). Something was evoked within Moses – his knowledge of God and his participation in God and his ways made him speak out beyond what he knew. Because he was close to God's heart, he expressed that heart in words that were his, but which had come from thoughts that were God's.

This is the beginning of something that I want to emphasise. I believe that God is helping us and leading us into prophetic praying. It is one of the most profound things that I have touched on in recent years, and the deeper we go into what it is about, the more mind-blowing it becomes. We must not be too aware of the distinction between prayer and prophecy, for, biblically, there is virtually no difference. When someone is prophesying to God accompanied by 'lyres, harps and cymbals' in 'giving thanks and praising the Lord' (1 Chronicles 25:1–3), he or she is obviously speaking to him, and so that is prayer.

As we saw earlier, Jesus calls prophesying to mountains and telling them to get into the sea prayer! When you speak 'horizontally' to a mountain, commanding it to throw itself into the sea in Jesus' name, you are speaking to that mountain prophetically, but Jesus says, 'Truly I say to you, if you have faith and do not doubt ... it will happen' (Matthew 21:21). A more dramatic example might be when Joshua speaks to the sun, saying 'sun be still!' (Joshua 10:12), and it is! Later on in the text we read that as Joshua prayed to God 'the Lord listened to the voice of a man', but Joshua is prophesying to the sun. Therefore prayer and prophecy are very closely woven together. God expressed this even more explicitly through Joel: 'It will come about after this that I will pour out My Spirit on all [hu]mankind and your sons and daughters will prophesy ...' (Joel 2:28). All flesh means all types: not just Jewish flesh but Gentile flesh also, not just male flesh but female flesh too: 'whoever calls on the name of the Lord will be delivered' (2:32). Prophesying is calling on the Lord.

That longing, that ache within Moses expressed itself through him because he was so close to God. I would like to point out that if Moses had been more concerned with his position in Israel rather than with God's heart for the people, or had been more concerned with his reputation as a prophet and only interested in the fact that God had chosen *him* to lead the people out of Egypt, he would never have said the words 'I would that *all* of God's people were prophets.' He would not have expressed God's heart in this prophetic way. Moses had a heart for all the people to prophesy because he had a heart for God and so shared God's heart.

Close to God's heart

If we are going to be prophetic we are going to have to be closer and closer to God's heart. This means that spontaneously, without even working it out, we must express what God is feeling. Contemporary Christianity is absolutely obsessed with us expressing what *we* are feeling, whereas we should be speaking out (even if it is in pain!) what is on *God's* heart. We need to be more concerned about God's emotions than our own! However, we cannot do this unless we spend time with him. There may be times as we pray in the Spirit when we, like Jesus in the garden of Gethsemane, will sweat, as it were, great drops of blood as we feel what God is feeling about a situation.

Prophecy began in the heartache of Moses. It expressed itself more consciously in the prophecy of Joel and when, at Pentecost, the prophecy of Joel was fulfilled and God poured out his Spirit, his sons and daughters prophesied and the church came into being. Prophecy is the instrument that God said was necessary if he was going to get his work done! If we are to take the good news into all the world, bring in the kingdom and prepare others to reign with him, we have to be a prophetic people. We must live close to the heart of God, and so sharing his feelings.

Prophetic prayer is never perfunctory prayer. Neither is it, necessarily, liturgical prayer. Sometimes it is helpful to use those beautiful prayers that we find in prayer books – they can be very useful to guide our intercession – but they are not necessarily prophetic prayers.

The mind of God

Prophetic prayer is not only eulogising and exalting the Lord. It is not only meditative prayer, where we think of the Lord Jesus and remember him – we have the Lord's table to help us to do that. Nor is prophetic prayer only worshipful prayer (although, of course, we can worship as we pray prophetically). Nor is it exactly thanksgiving prayer (although we are told to make our requests known 'with thanksgiving'). Prophetic prayer could contain supplication (and almost certainly will), and it could contain intercession, or incorporate 'words of knowledge'. All of these elements appear in what we are thinking of as prophetic prayer. But in the final analysis (without being finally definitive, as we are still feeling our way more deeply into this and do not know the final answer) the prophetic element appears to be one hundred per cent committed to and identified with God's mind. We know, of course, that the Holy Spirit has been given to us for this very purpose, for 'we do not know how to pray as we should' (Romans 8:26). This is not true in every case – sometimes we do know exactly what we want to pray for! – but we are speaking here about being so close to God's mind that we are expressing the thoughts that are inside God, not just our own ideas!

This is where it all becomes very deep. Sometimes, when we look at the Scriptures, it seems as if (for instance) Abraham and God are on two different sides of an argument (see Genesis 18:16–33). It is not really that they are on opposing sides, but that God is doing the most wonderful thing – he is taking us into his own internal counsels and he is using us in those counsels. It is there in the Old Testament specifically (see Amos 3:7; Jeremiah 23:18,20) and it is mind shattering! You will find it in the New Testament also. In John 17 Jesus talks to his Father in the upper room and the disciples are drawn into his conversation with the Father.

It is as if they are participating in the relationship between
the Father and the Son. The church, too, is brought into the
conversation as Jesus says:

> I do not ask on behalf of these alone, but for those also who
> believe in Me through their word; that they may all be one;
> even as You, Father, are in Me and I in You, that they also may
> be in Us, so that the world may believe that You sent Me ... I
> have made Your name known to them, and will make it
> known, so that the love with which You loved Me may be in
> them, and I in them.

Here we are actually getting into the very heartbeat of God
himself. This is where prophetic prayer comes from and it is
made possible by the gift of the Holy Spirit, specifically in
the New Testament sense, but also anticipated in those Old
Testament days. The Holy Spirit teaches us what to pray for
when we do not know what to ask and takes us into what
is going on inside God's heart.

In Romans 8:23–27 Paul explains:

> And not only this, but also we ourselves, having the first fruits
> of the Spirit, even we ourselves groan within ourselves, wait-
> ing eagerly for our adoption as sons, the redemption of our
> body. For in hope we have been saved, but hope that is seen is
> not hope; for who hopes for what he already sees? But if we
> hope for what we do not see, with perseverance we wait
> eagerly for it. In the same way the Spirit also helps our weak-
> ness; for we do not know how to pray as we should, but the
> Spirit Himself intercedes for us with groanings too deep for

words; and He who searches the hearts knows what the mind of the Spirit is, because He intercedes for the saints according to the will of God.

The Spirit is interceding for God's people within God's people, but the mind that the Spirit brings to us is God's mind. Here we see that Paul says rather a strange thing: that God 'knows his own mind'. God is looking at the Spirit in us (the church) and he sees his mind within the Spirit. I would suggest that a dialogue is going on within God the Father, God the Son and God the Holy Spirit, and what happens is that the Holy Spirit gets inside us and begins to pray beyond our feelings and beyond our understanding, but at the same time sharing our feelings and understanding. The debate within the Almighty is taking place within us. God is inside us by his Spirit and we are inside God as he interacts, Father, Son and Spirit. We need to understand this if we are going to understand some very difficult Scripture. The debate that is going on within God is being revealed to us in human language. This is why God ultimately had to become a man – human language is what makes communication between God and man possible, and human language is what God is using here, communicated by his Spirit as we pray.

Becoming what we are saying

Something wonderful happens when we are brought into the counsels of God. When God spoke to people in the Old

Testament days he used angels, as he still does sometimes today. The angel usually appeared in a human form if there was a message to communicate. For instance, a man of God appeared to Gideon and gave him God's message. It is possible, also, to have a man of God appear to you who is actually a man! Since the word 'angel' in both Hebrew and in Greek means 'messenger' we can think of a message given to us from God by either an angel or another human being.

Eventually, the man of God (or the angel) gets so caught up with the message that the two begin to merge into one – they become a prophet; message and messenger begin to assimilate. If you are going to be a prophet of anything worthwhile you have to begin to become what God is saying: God's word and God's messenger becoming one.

This is graphically portrayed when Ezekiel is told to eat the scroll on which is written the message he is to proclaim. As he ingests it, it becomes a part of him, and he a part of it. Ezekiel does not then impart the message as an instrument or a channel – he passes on the message because he has become what he is preaching! This is what is meant by 'becoming prophetic': becoming what you are saying and saying what you are becoming.

There are some other outstanding cases in the Bible. Hosea was totally identified with God's heart because he became (and felt) what God had become and felt. He was so identified with the message that he married a woman who turned out to be an adulteress. He then bought her back again from the slave market, forgave her, and tried to love her. Hosea was completely assimilated into God's message to the people – their behaviour towards God was like

that of an adulterous wife who had run away. But God
would still forgive and bring his people back. To Hosea, this
was no cerebral message that had just come into his mind
and been passed on to the people. When he spoke, his emotions were released, for he could identify with God's feelings through his own. As he prophesied he spoke as much
through his feelings as he did through his mind. The price
of being a prophet, for Hosea, was that his whole life was
taken up by God as he became the vehicle of God's speaking and God's expression.

The price that the church of God must pay in order to
be an instrument of sons and daughters prophesying and
therefore praying effectively (the two things are intimately
linked together, as we have seen) is that it becomes a
people whose whole lives are wrapped up with what God
is saying to the world and what God is wanting us to talk to
him about. Inevitably, the end product of this, as we get
more and more involved, is the incarnation. 'In the beginning was the Word, and the Word was with God, and the
Word was God ... And the Word became flesh, and dwelt
among us' (John 1:1,14).

God's history with his people in the Old Testament – his
process of communicating to them, giving them a language
whereby they could talk back to him without any hin-
drance – culminates in 'the Word'. In Jesus, God totally
identifies with humanity, completely and utterly expressing
his heart and his message. Even if there had been no expli-
cit references to the incarnation in the Old Testament, the
New Testament is the logical outworking of what God has
been doing since the days when he first spoke to Moses

through the angel in the burning bush. It was inevitable that God should become man. This is the kind of God that he is. The Jews should have expected him and been prepared to receive him! In the Old Testament God says some two hundred times or so that he wants to communicate by being with his people – 'I will be with you!' It was natural for him to one day become one of us.

There is nothing more logical than that through the stream of the Old Testament prophets the day would come when the ultimate prophetic instrument would appear – God himself, utterly identified, heart, soul, mind, everything, with humanity in Jesus.

God's heart in three prophets

1. Jeremiah

In Jeremiah 4:19 we notice that it is not easy to recognise whether it is Jeremiah or God who is speaking. It is not really important, since the prophet has become so closely identified with the heart of God, that when he opens his mouth, he expresses the things that are in God's own heart.

Once we are identified with God's heart and mind we notice that God takes up his prophets and his prophetic church and uses them to talk things through with himself! Please bear with me here; I am not trying to be blasphemous or irreverent. He is actually discussing things in himself with us. We are brought into the very counsels of God! The Lord is presented to us in the Bible as a God who talks

within himself. Most theology doesn't show us that, but the
Bible certainly does! Just as Jesus asked questions, God asks
questions – Jesus is the complete revelation of God.

Jeremiah 4:19–22 read:

> My soul, my soul! I am in anguish! Oh, my heart! My heart is
> pounding in me; I cannot be silent, because you have heard, O
> my soul, the sound of the trumpet, the alarm of war. Disaster
> on disaster is proclaimed, for the whole land is devastated; sud-
> denly my tents are devastated, my curtains in an instant. How
> long must I see the standard and hear the sound of the trum-
> pet? For My people are foolish, they know Me not; they are
> stupid children and have no understanding. They are shrewd to
> do evil, but to do good they do not know.

It seems at first that this cry is Jeremiah complaining about
the trumpet and the alarm of war. However, when we reach
Jeremiah 4:22, it becomes obvious that it is the Lord who is
speaking, for the 'people' are not Jeremiah's people – they
are God's people! God does not stand aloof, watching dis-
passionately from a distance, totally separate from all that is
going on. He himself hurts because of all that his people are
going through. Sometimes it seems as if the prophet and
God are having an argument. Next time you feel as if you
are arguing with God, please believe that it is not that you
are really arguing with him, but that you are participating in
the pain and the feelings of God. This is where prophetic
prayer is born!

This point is very important for us to understand. God is
not a static, distant God who saves or destroys at will. The

God of the Bible is so involved with us that when we cry out to him 'Oh God this should not be!' after something dreadful has happened he totally agrees with us. What is going on in our hearts is exactly what is going on in his heart as well – believe me! This is how the world is being spoken to. People who cry out to God are bringing God's heart to us: they are feeling just the same as he is about the things that are happening!

In Jeremiah 8:18–22 the prophet cries:

My sorrow is beyond healing, my heart is faint within me! Behold, listen! The cry of the daughter of my people from a distant land: 'Is the Lord not in Zion? Is her King not within her?' 'Why have they provoked me with their graven images, with foreign idols?' 'Harvest is past, summer is ended, and we are not saved.' For the brokenness of the daughter of my people I am broken; I mourn, dismay has taken hold of me. Is there no balm in Gilead? Is there no physician there? Why then has not the health of the daughter of my people been restored?'

God is speaking through the prophet. God himself is asking the question: 'Why is there no balm in Gilead?' There should have been healing but there was none. God is hurt as well as us that because of many things beyond our understanding, because of idolatry and sin, healing has not come. This is not because God does not care. But here is prophetic praying, and it can change things very radically, as we shall see. In Jeremiah 10:19–22 the prophet cries out yet again:

Woe is me, because of my injury! My wound is incurable. But I said, 'Truly this is a sickness, and I must bear it.' My tent is destroyed, and all my ropes are broken; my sons have gone from me and are no more. There is no one to stretch out my tent again or to set up my curtains. For the shepherds have become stupid and have not sought the Lord; therefore they have not prospered, and all their flock is scattered. The sound of a report! Behold, it comes – a great commotion out of the land of the north – to make the cities of Judah a desolation, a haunt of jackals.

It is almost impossible to separate Jeremiah from the Lord here because they are so closely identified.

We can take this further. Jeremiah 12:5 says: 'If you have run with footmen and they have tired you out, then how can you compete with horses? If you fall down in a land of peace, how will you do in the thicket of the Jordan?' God is saying to Jeremiah, 'You have not managed to keep up with me this far – so how are you going to keep up when things are more difficult still?' In other words, 'If you are complaining that things are too painful for you now, what will happen when your suffering increases? If you cease to go on being involved in the anguish in my heart and in what I feel, then you will no longer be a prophet.'

This point is emphasised more strongly in Jeremiah 15:19–21.

Therefore, thus says the Lord, 'If you return, then I will restore you – before Me you will stand; and if you extract the precious from the worthless, you will become My spokesman. They for their part may turn to you, but as for you, you must not turn to them. Then I will make you to this people a fortified wall of bronze; and though they fight against you, they will not prevail over you; for I am with you to save you and deliver you,' declares the Lord. 'So I will deliver you from the hand of the wicked, and I will redeem you from the grasp of the violent.'

The promise is given to Jeremiah that if he keeps running with the horsemen and then with the chariots, if he pays the price to go on being the very vehicle of God's message and his spokesman into the world, then God will sustain and strengthen him. But he must be aware that if God is going to be rejected so will he be! This is why when Jeremiah says that he was 'like a gentle lamb led to the slaughter' (11:19) he uses terminology that the book of Revelation uses for Jesus (Revelation 5:6). Why? Because when Jeremiah was rejected and led to the slaughter it was as if God was being rejected, which indeed he was, because Jeremiah was the embodiment of God's heart and mind. It is a valid hermeneutic to apply this prophetic statement to Jesus in the New Testament. In the Old Testament God says 'you made me "bear" with your iniquities'. Exactly the same word is used for the 'bearing' of the scapegoat; for the 'bearing' of sin that is used in the sacrifices; and for the 'bearing' that Jesus took upon himself on the cross, which we see prophesied in Isaiah 53:4.

2. Abraham

In Genesis 22:1–2 we read:

> Now it came about after these things, that God tested Abraham, and said to him, 'Abraham!' And he said, 'Here I am.' He said, 'Take now your son, your only son, whom you love, Isaac, and go to the land of Moriah, and offer him there as a burnt offering on one of the mountains of which I will tell you.'

Abraham, as we know, takes his son and journeys to the place the Lord had told him about and prepares to sacrifice him. In 22:11–12, however, we read:

> But the angel of the Lord called to him from heaven and said, 'Abraham, Abraham!' And he said, 'Here I am.' He said, 'Do not stretch out your hand against the lad, and do nothing to him; for now I know that you fear God, since you have not withheld your son, your only son, from Me.'

If this language means anything at all it tells us that there was a time when God did not know that Abraham feared him! Now that God has seen Abraham and Isaac on the top of the mount he *does* know. It is important that we understand what this means. What is the point of praying unless there is some way in which true conversation with God can take place? In other words, if God says to us, 'Perhaps', we can talk back and say, 'Well, perhaps not, Lord.' Or, if God says, 'I don't know,' we can speak to him saying, 'We think it would be this. Let's try it!'

Such actions begin to make our prayer life, our conversation with God, prophetic. Here is a realistic changing of things. Most of us know that Abraham is the first person named in the Bible as a prophet. In Genesis 20:17, when he prays for the household of Abimelech in order that the women should once more produce children, he does not pray for Abimelech out of his own experience, because his experience is quite the reverse. Sarah was unable to have children at this time. It is the height of arrogance to believe that you cannot pray for someone because you have not been through what they have experienced. Abraham prayed for Abimelech out of the word of God. Abraham was called a prophet, he prayed, and the women were once again able to conceive, even though Abraham himself had not received an answer to his decades of prayer for the birth of Isaac. God, speaking to Abimelech in 20:7, says (of Abraham): 'Now therefore, restore the man's wife, for he is a prophet, and he will pray for you and you will live.' What was it that had made Abraham a prophet? In Genesis 18 Abraham had prayed for Sodom. Here is a prophet in the making. This is probably the reason why God was able to call him a prophet by chapter 20!

In 18:17 God said, 'Shall I hide from Abraham what I am about to do?' The answer was, of course, that he would not, because one day he would want to write Amos 3:7: 'Surely the Lord God does nothing unless He reveals His secret counsel to His servants the prophets.' It seems in the history of the human race to be a necessity that humankind co-operates with God, otherwise he does nothing of ultimate consequence! God is forever looking for someone to come into his heart in order that the person should start to speak and pray prophetically.

God says, therefore (Genesis 18:18–19):

> Abraham will surely become a great and mighty nation, and in him all the nations of the earth will be blessed? For I have chosen him, so that he may command his children and his household after him to keep the way of the Lord by doing righteousness and justice, so that the Lord may bring upon Abraham what He has spoken about him.

Supposing that God had not had this conversation with Abraham? Presumably he would not have been able to bring about for Abraham what he had spoken about with him.

> And the Lord said, 'The outcry of Sodom and Gomorrah is indeed great, and their sin is exceedingly grave. I will go down now, and see if they have done entirely according to its outcry, which has come to Me; and if not, I will know' (Genesis 18:20–21).

Here is the Lord gleaning information – 'I will go down and see if it is true.' Verses 22–24 continue:

> The men turned away from there and went toward Sodom, while Abraham was still standing before the Lord. Abraham came near and said, 'Will You indeed sweep away the righteous with the wicked? Suppose there are fifty righteous within the city; will You indeed sweep it away and not spare the place for the sake of the fifty righteous who are in it?'

God must have known that there were not fifty righteous people in the city! I want to suggest that this is a sign of the dialogue that is taking place within God and which is now going on in Abraham. God has now brought Abraham in on his talking about this situation within himself. God does not want to destroy the city! Of course, we know that he does destroy it – but God's heart does not want to do what he knows he will ultimately have to do if there is no repentance. Here lies the confusion that often arises. We think that we are more righteous than God as we talk back to him and say, 'Surely you will not destroy it if there are even fifty righteous there?' What is happening is that God is giving us the most wonderful privilege possible: he is taking his prophets into his counsel chambers and making them part of it. God is talking now, within himself, with us! I believe that the Lord wants to emphasise this in our prophetic and prayer life in these last days as we break through into the final movement of the kingdom of God throughout the earth. Abraham says: 'Far be it from You to do such a thing, to slay the righteous with the wicked, so that the righteous and the wicked are treated alike. Far be it from You! Shall not the Judge of all the earth deal justly?' (Genesis 18:25). Do we think that God does not know this? It is not as though the Lord is reluctant to save the city. Those who are in the prophetic calling, know that when they talk like this with God they are talking out of the basis of what he has already put in their hearts. Even an atheist could deduce this, for when an atheist says 'If I were God I would have done this, that, or the other' what he or she is really saying is that he or she is judging God by his or her own (presumed) superior righteousness. By definition, however, no one can have a

superior righteousness to that of God. The atheist is also assum-
ing that his or her love is superior to God's love, but from
where did he or she get this idea of love if not from what it
ultimately is? We are back to God again!

Abraham speaks up again in 18:27–28, saying 'Now
behold, I have ventured to speak to the Lord, although I am
but dust and ashes. Suppose the fifty righteous are lacking
five, will You destroy the whole city because of five?' By
18:32–33 he is saying "'Oh may the Lord not be angry, and I
shall speak only this once; suppose ten are found there?" And
He said, "I will not destroy it on account of the ten." As soon
as He had finished speaking to Abraham the Lord departed,
and Abraham returned to his place.' But in Genesis 19, as we
know, the Lord judges Sodom. There are times when God
does have to judge the human race. And he has to judge us
in order to get the cancer out of the whole human system.
Sometimes that means that the innocent die along with the
unjust and that children perish with the mature sinners. There
are times when God can do nothing else.

Abraham had asked for ten righteous people to save the
city, but he could only find three or four. Even then, God
sent an angelic presence into the city to bring Lot and his
family out. I feel certain that if Abraham had not prayed
these angels would not have been sent.

3. Moses

Read about Moses, another great pray-er, in Exodus
32:6–11.

Moses rejects the idea that the people are his people and says to God: 'They are your people, you brought them out!' Who is right? Is God right, or Moses? When God says 'Leave me alone' I do not think that it is that he is saying 'I don't want you to talk to me, Moses.' He did say that to Jeremiah – not that Jeremiah took any notice; he was too much into the prophetic swing of things by then! Was that disobedience to God? Well, Jeremiah went on praying, even though he was told not to. Perhaps God said 'Leave me alone' because he was so hurt, so grieved by the people's behaviour, just as we want to be by ourselves when we have been pained and hurt.[2]

Moses does not leave God alone to destroy the people. Instead he puts three very good reasons to the Lord why he should not destroy them! 'Why does Your anger burn against Your people whom You have brought out from the land of Egypt with great power and with a mighty hand?' (32:11). 'Why should the Egyptians speak, saying, "With evil intent He brought them out ...?"' (32:12). 'Remember Abraham, Isaac, and Israel, Your servants to whom You swore by Yourself, and said to them, "I will multiply your descendants as the stars of the heavens ..."' (32:13). God already knew all these reasons why he should not destroy the children of Israel. In fact, he probably knew one or two other arguments besides! What is important is that God has got somebody else sharing his heart. It seems that if he can't get someone else to share his heart then he cannot do, ultimately, what he wants: that which is for the benefit and the final destiny of

---

[2] cf Fretheim 'The Suffering of God'

the human race. This is not a do-it-yourself business: it is God in relationship with people whereby his word is coming through.

Look at 32:14: 'So the Lord changed His mind about the harm which He said He would do to His people.' God changed his mind! If this exchange on the top of the mountain had not taken place between Moses and God the Lord would have destroyed the people.

Conclusion

The future and the destiny of the human race, or of our own little part of it, depends upon this kind of praying: the kind that changes God's mind. Not changes it in the sense that he never wanted to do something in the first place, but changes it so as to put him in the place where he can do something different, changes his course of action because of his co-operation with us. This co-operation with us is a praying co-operation. If we do not learn how to pray, if we are not those who are living closer and closer to God's heart so that his heart is coming out through us, then we are not going to contribute much to the great commission and final world evangelisation.

A wonderful example of all that I have been saying is found in Amos 3:7: 'Surely the Lord God does nothing unless He reveals His secret counsel to His servants the prophets.' Also in Jeremiah 23:18 we read: 'But who has stood in the council of the Lord, that he should see and hear His word?' and in verse 22: 'But if they had stood in My council, then they would have announced My words to My people, and would have turned them back from their evil way and from the evil of their deeds.' There is a council of God where God's communications, God's conversations, are taking place, both within God himself, Father, Son and Holy Spirit, and with those who are allowed in there, like the prophets. When Amos (in chapter 7) has a vision of the locust swarm that will destroy the grain just as the second crop is coming up and cries out to the Lord on behalf of Jacob, the Lord relents. 'This will not happen,' he says. He changes his mind. When God then shares his intention to judge Israel by fire Amos cries out again, saying: 'Lord God, I beg you, stop!' Once more the Lord relents: 'This will not happen either,' he says. We can see a changing of God's mind through Amos's prayers.

There is a great need for prophetic praying that allows God to do the things that he ultimately wants to do. There is a need for prophetic praying so that we can touch the heart of God in all its aspects, even the different sides of it that debate and share together. It is from men and women who get to know God at that depth and who want to get deeper and deeper into him that the opportunity to bring about the final exaltation of our Lord Jesus Christ will come.

5

Word and Prayer
by Faith Forster

There are many aspects of the Christian life that need attention if we are to grow in our relationship with God. We might look at how the Holy Spirit works in our hearts so that we grow and expand within to contain more of the life of Jesus. We might consider our need to fellowship together as the body of Christ.

But what I want to emphasise now is prayer and the word of God, the basic disciplines at the heart of the Christian life. I have been a Christian for more years than I can remember, but I still find that my spiritual life has to keep coming back to these basics. I may develop in a certain area – intercession, understanding the word, exercising spiritual gifts – but I still have to keep underpinning it all with the disciplines that strengthen my relationship with the Lord. Discipline is an important part of any relationship. Without it, we start to neglect, dishonour or abuse the other person. We need to work on our devotional life, to develop something like the old idea of the 'quiet time'. We need the discipline of a time with God each day, a time of finding freshness with him.

Prayer

Prayer is the way we touch God, the way we begin our spiritual lives. If you are a Christian but have never prayed aloud you need to start doing it because, as it says in Scripture, 'everyone who calls on the name of the Lord will be saved' (Acts 2:21). You do not have to shout your head off (although I am sure some spiritual groups think that you do!) but you do have to speak aloud. Some people say that you can pray in your head, and of course you can – but in your head you can also wander. Someone's prayer life may be in his or her head because circumstances require it: maybe he or she shares a room with six other people and cannot pray aloud very easily without the roommates all knowing what is being prayed about. But even so, it is good to learn how to pray aloud, because you will find that this helps you to focus and be specific. So, if you have not prayed aloud before, make sure you do so today! You can do it on your own or with others. When you pray aloud you can really see what is in your heart because what is hidden inside comes out. The mouth is where the heart comes out into the open, where the spirit is revealed. It is when we pray aloud that we find out how much faith we have got, how much love we have, or how much unbelief or lack of love – and then we can ask the Lord to deal with it!

There is one barrier we always have to overcome when we talk about prayer – guilt! We've got to start praying that God will rid us of guilt in our lives in every way, not just in the area of prayer, because guilt is a barrier to prayer. It is not just the *result* of prayerlessness; it is the *barrier* that causes prayerlessness. So let us get rid of guilt right at the start. Every one of us at times finds prayer difficult, or we find certain types of prayer difficult, but as we meditate on what the Scriptures say about prayer we can discover how to get better at it.

Four types of prayer

In 1 Timothy 2:1 Paul says that there are four different kinds of prayer that should be prayed at all times. I would like to term these petitions and supplications, prayers (from the Greek *proseuche*, which means to pour out; therefore I would like to call this kind of prayer 'outpourings'), intercessions and thanksgivings.

1. Petitions and supplications

Supplication simply means 'humble petition': we ask God for something specific. In that word 'petition' there is a hint of agreement, a little bit like when we make a petition to an MP and we get as many people as possible to sign it. One of the most helpful things in corporate times of prayer is to pour out your hearts to God together and then seek to formulate a specific request to God: something that you are going to agree on together to ask him for. In the outpouring stage, you find that all your unbelief starts to manifest. If I start praying prayers aloud I find whether I really believe them. It is hard to keep up that religious 'Of course, God, I

know you can do anything whatever' when you are praying
aloud in front of people. But then as you begin to pour out
your heart you may find that God begins to help you formulate a request. Something rises up within you, you want
to pray specifically, you want to ask God: 'May I see some
sign or indication for good in this situation?' This is a very
simple thing to ask and very often I begin praying like this.
'Lord, give me some encouragement that I am praying in
the right direction.' This may be a small encouragement.
Perhaps I am praying for a person and I notice that they
have softened and something begins to change, and I think,
'Wonderful! God has answered that specific prayer: now I
can pray further along that line.'

In this way we use our petitions. Jesus surely referred to
the wonder of petitions when he said (Matthew 18:19): 'if
two of you agree on earth about anything that they may ask,
it shall be done for them by My Father who is in heaven'.
We will find that agreements together in prayer are very
powerful. But when we pray in agreement we need to be
really honest with our hearts. If someone were to ask me to
agree with them concerning something, but then prayed for
£5000 by the end of the week, it is not really right just to
say 'Yes, yes, I agree, I agree' when maybe in my heart I am
thinking 'Chance would be a fine thing!' Agreement is
deeper than this. If I am not sure that I agree I should say:
'Hang on a minute, I'm not sure I've got faith to ask for
that, so could we just look at it for a minute? What are we
really asking for? What do we need that for?' We need to
formulate clear petitions and we need to have a look at any
unbelief in our hearts because this needs to be dealt with by

God. Maybe our petition needs changing. Perhaps we are asking wrongly. James says: 'You ask and you have not because you ask amiss.' We do not want to ask wrong things. When we 'ask amiss' we may not be asking anything evil. James surely meant that, when I ask for something for myself, this is selfish prayer. I do not always get selfish prayers answered – do you? This is a very good thing, really. I have found that God is so eager to bless that lots of prayers I pray get answered, even the very small things. God is wonderful like that. But every now and then one doesn't get answered and it brings me up short. Then I look at it and I think 'Goodness, I have got awfully selfish in my praying.' At times I start to use God like a slot machine – I put the prayers in and he delivers! But this is not who God is, and he will not let you use him like this all the time.

2. Outpourings

So what are outpourings? In some ways it is very easy to pour out your heart. A few weeks ago I was talking at a meeting about conflict. At the end of the meeting a young man came up to me and said: 'I'm actually not a Christian. I've been brought here by a friend. I've got a situation of conflict in my family and I wondered if you could help me or advise me or something.' He began to tell me about a conflict he was having with his brother that he desperately wanted to resolve. He really wanted to be in relationship with his brother. He began to pour out his problem, and I gave him whatever helpful advice God had given me over the years.

I said to him, 'You know, I guess in the end I have found that when I have difficulties and conflicts in relationships they are never really solved unless I bring it to God in prayer. God is the relational God, he knows how to heal relationships.' I asked him if we could pray about this.

'Well, yes, I would be glad to if it would help,' he said.

'So why don't *you* pray about it?' I said.

'Oh, I've never prayed aloud,' he replied. 'I wouldn't know how to!'

'Well,' I said, 'you know how you have been talking to me about what is in your heart? You talked with great sincerity because you really wanted to resolve this situation. You can talk to God just like that. He is here with us, so why not just tell him what is in your heart?'

'All right then,' he said, and he did.

Having not prayed before, even to find salvation, he started to pray and tell God about the real pain that was in his heart. He poured out his heart and I have no doubt that God heard him. Outpourings are not the only kind of prayer, but they are an important kind of prayer.

I would include speaking in tongues in outpourings. Some of you might say, 'Oh, I don't speak in tongues.' That's fine. But if we ask the Holy Spirit to come and fill us we know that one of the spiritual gifts, and one very frequently mentioned in the New Testament, is speaking in tongues. Paul says that the one who speaks in a tongue edifies him or herself, builds him or herself up. This is a pretty good reason to speak in tongues. Paul also says that when we pray in a tongue we are praying in the Spirit. Those of us who can and do speak in tongues can use our tongues to pour out our hearts — our spirit is communicating, with the help of the Holy Spirit, directly with the Father. Quite often, if I do not know how to pray, I start praying in tongues. This is another way in which we can build ourselves up. But I have found that the Holy Spirit is not content to let me speak in tongues forever. You might think speaking in tongues is the most spiritual way to pray, but I do not think that the Bible says so. I think that this is the way to pour out the heart, but the Holy Spirit is all the time trying to press us to make specific petitions to God, because as we make specific petition we know whether our prayers are answered.

3. Intercessions

Intercessions are the third kind of prayer. The word literally means 'go between'. I like to think of intercession as exactly that — a 'going between'. Sometimes it is a 'going between' a person or a situation and God — I might stand up on your behalf and plead with God for you. This is interceding. The word 'intercede' in the Old Testament is *paga*, which means 'to strike against'. An intercession is quite a strong prayer. We are really going to lay hold in prayer. Very often intercession is strengthened by fasting. If you are going to have the spiritual energy that intercession needs, you often need to gain it through denying the flesh. This is a funny paradox, is it not? You get spiritual energy through fasting; you get physical energy through eating. Sometimes we need physical energy and other times we need spiritual energy. Intercession needs spiritual energy.

When we see a drastic situation, for example, the potential eruption of violence, we feel the need to pray for those who will be affected. We feel the need to go between them and God and say: 'Lord, have mercy – spare, deliver!' At other times we might go between a person or a situation and the enemy, because we recognise that there is a direct oppression by the enemy. We might say: 'I resist you, Satan, in Jesus' name.' I love the biography of James Fraser, who went out to China in the early 1900's. He saw a wonderful move of God amongst the Lisu people. When he was learning how to pray for these people to come to Christ he discovered within the first couple of years that they were so bound up in paganism, occult practices and demonic powers that the only way he could pray effectively for them was to resist those powers around them. He records in his journal that he would walk up and down as he prayed and say: 'The blood of Jesus Christ has overcome,' or 'For this the Son of God is manifest to destroy the works of the devil.' He would speak out the word of God against the demonic powers that were holding the Lisu people. God began to break the Lisu free from demonic bondage and there was a wonderful turning to the Lord amongst them.

4. Thanksgivings

The fourth type of prayer is thanksgiving prayer. This also requires that spiritual energy we talked about earlier. Thanksgivings are a lovely kind of prayer, but we often forget to pray them. We need to give thanks to God. He is such a wonderful God. He answers prayer! As we give thanks we actually open our heart to God to receive more from him. Often we do not receive more from God because we do not give him thanks. We should therefore get into the habit of giving thanks to God for prayers answered. We should not just take this for granted. As well as thanking God for prayers that have been answered we need to give him thanks for who he is. This can be done as you present your case to God. Philippians 4:6 says: 'Be anxious for nothing, but in everything by prayer and supplication with *thanksgiving* let your requests be made known to God.' Paul is saying: 'When you ask God for something, make sure you are thanking him.' You might say: 'Thank you, Lord, because you are a prayer-answering God. Thank you, Lord, I know you hear me.' This is what Jesus did when he prayed for Lazarus in John 11. If we give thanks even as we pray, our hearts become more open in faith to God, and we make room for those around us to grow in faith too.

So there we have four kinds of prayer. This can help us when we come to pray and we do not seem to have any spiritual energy. We can begin by pouring out our hearts to God, and as we do so maybe he will pour the specific petition we need into our hearts so that we can offer it to him. We can give him thanks and begin to worship and thus find ourselves empowered to push forward more in intercession. This is how I find it works. Fasting is not the only way of gaining spiritual strength, you will be glad to know! As we worship and give thanks to God, declaring his word, we grow stronger to intercede.

When the disciples approached Jesus and said 'Lord, teach us to pray' I understand from this that they, like us, thought 'I just don't know how to pray like Jesus does.' I'm guessing they watched Jesus go out and pray for hours and they thought, 'Gosh, I have a job to keep going for three or four minutes!' In answer, Jesus firstly taught the disciples the Lord's Prayer. We will look later at the Lord's Prayer as a pattern for prayer to help us as we structure a time with God. Secondly, he told them a parable. Read Luke 11:1–13.

Let us learn some principles of prayer from Jesus' parable. Firstly, we see that prayer grows out of *relationship*. The word 'friend' keeps arising in the parable. The man can ask for the loaves because of the relationship. Effective prayer arises out of relationships. We want to get to know God because in our relationship with him we know we can call on him not only in a crisis but for all the needs of our lives.

Secondly, we see *petition* in action – 'lend me three loaves' – you can't get more specific than that, can you? The friend didn't ask 'What have you got in the cupboard?' – he said 'lend me three loaves'. The request is very specific, and it is granted. Through this parable Jesus invites us to be specific. If we ask the Holy Spirit to help us we can formulate specific petitions that are in line with God's heart for us.

Thirdly, the prayer is *compassionate*. The friend was not asking for the loaves to feed himself, but for an unexpected visitor. He had nothing to feed his friend, but he wanted to feed him. When our prayers become totally self-centred, God starts to challenge. He starts to bring people with greater needs than ours along. We need to have compassion in our hearts to pray for our friends when they are in need, but also to pray for those who may not be our friends but who are our neighbours in the world. People need our prayers, so compassion needs to be part of our prayer life. Very often we do not really pray for people because we do not feel touched by their infirmities – but Jesus does, and we can ask him to put that compassion in our hearts, because this will strengthen our prayer. Compassion strengthens prayer – not emotion, but compassion. Emotion may sometimes strengthen and sometimes weaken prayer, but real compassion, which is in the heart, brings strength to our prayer.

Fourthly, prayer is *humble*. This does not preclude *boldness*. The friend's request was granted because of his boldness. One of the incredible things about prayer is that we can be both bold and humble. Perhaps boldness is the other side of the coin to humility, because if you know you have nothing and you are totally dependent on God, then you can be bold in asking him. Jesus encouraged us to be bold. The word he uses for 'boldness' in verse 8 actually means 'shamelessness' in Greek. The man did not mind hammering on the door at midnight and saying 'I need it, I need it now' even though his friend was in bed. There was a shamelessness about his actions; there was a confidence, an absolute assurance: 'This guy will give me what I want, partly because he is my friend, but even more so because I am hammering on the door and it is midnight. If I keep hammering long enough he will answer.' This may be shameless, but Jesus commends these actions. When you are in a crisis he doesn't want you to think, 'Oh dear, poor me, it's all gone wrong again, what can I do?' He wants you to be bold and say, 'OK God, it's gone wrong – I need you, Lord.' Such prayer does not have to be arrogant: it can arise out of real humility. It is persistent prayer. This is why Jesus goes on and expands it: 'So ask, ask, ask and it shall be given you, seek, seek, seek and you will find.' The verbs are continuous, indicating repeated action: we need to keep bringing things to God in prayer, often. This is not because he is reluctant to answer, but because this builds our faith. Continual asking starts to break through those things that hinder our faith, and faith is a great key to answered prayer. Faith is also a gift of the Spirit, so we need our prayers to be empowered by the Spirit, guided by the Spirit and given focus and direction by the Spirit. This is why Jesus said: 'Well, you are asking for gifts and your father wants to give them, so he will first give you the Holy Spirit.' This guidance of the Holy Spirit is the most important thing to ask for. This is where humility comes in: we cannot even pray without the help of the Spirit. Even my deepest pleadings and beggings are not effective if I do not have the Holy Spirit in my heart.

The devotional Lord's Prayer

We need to have a certain time, preferably every day, when we have a specific time with God – devotional time. There may be lots of occasions in the day when you pray. You may be praying as you are driving around or as you are walking. You may pray as you walk the dog; you may join prayer meetings and pray with others. But there needs to be a time when you engage specifically with God and in that time lay hold of the word of God. Many people find it difficult to know what they are actually going to do when they take time with God. Some can take half an hour or an hour with God first thing in the morning. If you cannot, do it when you can. When my kids were small they used to have a doze at lunchtime and that was often when I would take the time to be with God – it was a time that I could be on my own. You may have to be creative about finding time, but if you can, pray first thing in the morning. Even if you only take ten or fifteen minutes you will find it an enormous help in your day. If you can take half an hour, wonderful. If you can take an hour, even better. But let us ask God to help us, however much time we have.

I found it useful to structure devotional time around the Lord's Prayer. The following formula can be adapted for a ten or fifteen minute devotional time, or, if you have an hour, it can be expanded. Look at the Prayer Clock below. The prayer breaks naturally into specific phrases and each phrase can be used to lead us in our prayer. 'WITBRED' can be used as a mnemonic to help in remembering the different aspects of the prayer, and this will help to structure your devotional time. Firstly, it is helpful to pray through the whole prayer, to focus your heart and mind, and then begin to take it phrase by phrase.

PRAYER CLOCK

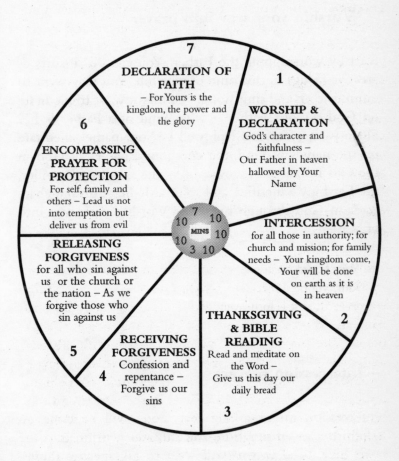

7
DECLARATION OF FAITH
– For Yours is the kingdom, the power and the glory

1
WORSHIP & DECLARATION
God's character and faithfulness –
Our Father in heaven hallowed by Your Name

6
ENCOMPASSING PRAYER FOR PROTECTION
For self, family and others – Lead us not into temptation but deliver us from evil

INTERCESSION
for all those in authority; for church and mission; for family needs – Your kingdom come, Your will be done on earth as it is in heaven

RELEASING FORGIVENESS
for all who sin against us or the church or the nation – As we forgive those who sin against us

7
10 10
MINS
10 10
3 10

2
THANKSGIVING & BIBLE READING
Read and meditate on the Word –
Give us this day our daily bread

5
RECEIVING FORGIVENESS
Confession and repentance –
Forgive us our sins

4

3

'Our Father who is in heaven,
Hallowed be Your name.'

– Worship your way into prayer

Start by worshipping the Father. You can do all sorts of
creative things in this time of worship. You may want to
put music on and sing along, you might want to meditate
on God as your Father – what kind of a Father is he?
Since we are praying 'hallowed be Your name', meditate
on the names of God, the compound names of God in
the Old Testament: Jehovah Jireh, the Lord my Provider,
the Lord my Sanctifier, and so on. Meditate on the character of God through his name. Worship your way into
prayer.

'Your kingdom come.
Your will be done,
on earth as it is in heaven.'

– Intercession prayers

Intercession means asking that God's will be done on
earth in a given situation. You can add petition into the
mix here, because you will want to ask specific things.
Very often we will start the day by praying 'Lord, you

know I have got this very important lecture to give' or 'I have got this important person to see' or 'I'm worried about my child in school.' We immediately think about our own concerns. Jesus knows that we do this, and so he shows us how to go from worship straight into intercession. You might want to pray not only for yourself and your family but also for your church and your nation, or for many nations. Whatever you have on your heart, pray for it now. Intercede!

'Give us this day our daily bread.'

– Thanksgiving and Bible reading

I think that this phrase has two connotations. Our daily bread is God's provision for our physical needs. Generally, we can live day by day, we do have enough to eat, we do have air to breathe and God is gracious, so we should start by giving him thanks for his graciousness and provision. 'Thank you, Lord, that you provide for us, thank you that you do give us our needs each day. You give us bodily strength for the new day too.' But then we also remember that Jesus said 'Man shall not live on bread alone, but on every word that proceeds out of the mouth of God' (Matthew 4:4). Therefore this phrase also serves as a reminder that God has given me another sort of daily bread – that manna from heaven in the form of his word. So it is at this point that I read the Scriptures, because this flows out of worship and intercession and thanksgiving. There are times when I get so caught up in this part that I leave the rest of the Lord's Prayer for another day. That's OK: this is why I pray the whole prayer through first at the beginning.

How do you approach the element of Bible reading? In my experience, if you do not have anything in your mind as to what you are going to read in the Bible today, you will either just flick it open and see what comes up, or you will turn to the psalms. But it is helpful, sometimes, to have a little bit of structure in your mind, otherwise you will find that your Bible diet is all the same all the time. This is nice for a while, but you need a bit of variation! Therefore I have tried to do different things. I have a one-year Bible. I used to use the one-year Living Bible, and I found it very refreshing for a couple of years. The language is easy and it approaches the Scriptures with a fresh perspective on the word of God. But I find that I can never stay away very long from a more accurate translation of some kind. The New International Version does a good one-year Bible. For every day of the year you will find a passage from the Old Testament, a passage from the New Testament, a psalm and a proverb. You get a very balanced diet and work through the whole Bible in a year. Nice and easy – you just put your marker in and you turn to the next set of passages. So that is one helpful way in which you can vary your biblical diet.

Another way is to follow some of the wonderful Bible reading notes you can get. I have been looking at some of the Scripture Union notes recently. Instead of carrying your Bible around, readings are printed out for you in magazine format: the biblical passage is just printed on the page with a comment underneath. I imagine that Bible reading notes would suit many busy people's lifestyles, so why not try them? The most important thing is to get the word of God into you. Whatever works best for you – start there. I do believe that we need to get more seriously into the word of God. Let us find any way we can to get something of the word of God into us each day.

'And forgive us our debts,
as we also have forgiven our debtors.'

– Receive and Release forgiveness

Bring your own sins to the Lord. Keep short accounts with him. Think about those you need to forgive and ask him to forgive you and to help you to forgive others. Fully releasing forgiveness to those who have hurt us can be a daily choice – not to hold the grudge but to give it up to God.

'And do not lead us into temptation,
but deliver us from evil.'

– Encompassing prayers

The Celtic Prayer of Encircling is a useful image to help us pray here. Simply imagine that you are drawing a circle around yourself (sometimes the Celtic saints literally used to draw a circle around themselves) and see it as the presence of God encircling you and protecting you. It is an encompassing prayer: as the Psalmist speaks out, 'You have enclosed me behind and before' (Psalm 139:5). I think that when we pray 'deliver us from evil' we are praying not only for ourselves but for those we love and those God puts in our hearts. Pray encompassing prayers – pray that the name of Jesus and the Spirit of God will surround and protect you today.

'For Yours is the kingdom
and the power and the glory
forever. Amen.'

– Declaration of faith

Use one of the verses you have read in the Bible as your declaration of faith back to God, or perhaps say, 'Yours is the kingdom, Lord, and the power and the glory for ever!' Romans 10:17 tells us that 'faith comes from hearing, and hearing by the word of Christ' and it is good to finish our prayer time in faith for the coming day. As we speak out

words of Christ we find faith rises in our hearts —
whatever we face currently, it is put into the perspective of
the eternal kingdom of our God, his power and his glory.
Amen!

6

Praying 'Bible Prayers'

Whatever we do, however we read the Bible, we must keep praying, because when we turn to the word of God we are meant to read it prayerfully. God is communicating with you and you can hear him coming alive to you in your current situation through the instrument that he has given us: his words spoken and recorded through history – the Bible. It is always good and useful to have a Bible around somewhere.

When I was in the Air Force I had three bibles. One I carried in an attaché case. I had another on my desk to show people where I stood. Not that I often stood on my desk, but you know what I mean. I also carried a little Bible in my tunic pocket, especially made for that purpose, so I could whip it out at any time – after all, the Queen's Regulations say that officers are to encourage men in religion! As I lectured, students were always asking questions about my faith to divert me from my subject. On one occasion when I was asked a question I bent down, took the Bible out of my attaché case, standing on one side of the room, and used it to answer the question. That raised a second question, so I went to my desk, and answered the question from the Bible I kept there. I was just walking to the back of the room when I was asked a third question – I took my third Bible out of my pocket. At this point, the well-known atheist of the group threw his hands up in the air and said, 'Blimey, I give in! He's got bibles everywhere!' The Bible is a very useful instrument for putting the fear of something into somebody! More than this, if you keep talking into it, you will find that God is communicating back and you've got some answers to some difficult questions. They won't all be obvious: we need to dig them out through prayerful study. Perhaps we need reminding, in these days, of the purpose and the nature of the Bible and how to read it.

The Bible is like an incomplete play. There are supposed to be five acts, but you have only got acts one, two, three and five. Act four is missing. Acts one, two and three are the beginning of the story. Act five finishes the story off. Act four is set inbetween and is where we live today – the church age. We need to listen directly to the Holy Spirit, who is guiding us into all truth. We need to get to know the main character, Jesus, and the things he has done. As we read the first three acts we get to know the plot, the characters and something about how the piece is being directed. But we can also communicate directly with the author/director and ask him to tell us more about the story so that we can play our part well in act four. So many Christians do not participate in the real story – they wander around, acting out their own sub-plots. But if we do not play our part right in act four, how will it flow into the remainder of the story? How will act five fit? We want to hasten the day of the Lord by getting on with the story. We mustn't try to upstage the main character. We are to be as supporting actors, supporting the chief player – Jesus. Jesus is the reason we want to get through the story. We want Jesus to say 'Wasn't that a great play? Wasn't that a great story?' But most of the time we upstage him and say 'What a marvellous ministry I've got. My ministry is so important – I do so many good things for God.' Yet if we were living as God intended us to live we would be getting this play moving to where God wants it. He has already written the last chapter: Jesus is coming again!

So we must seek to live out this play to make it complete. That is why the Bible is so necessary. We cannot really get to know the main character; we can't really understand the past; we can't possibly know or even guess where the plot is going unless we use the Bible.

The Bible is very much like Jesus. Jesus is the word of God. Some have made a big distinction between Jesus and the Bible: they say that Jesus is the word and the Bible is not. I don't think they are right. The Bible is very much like Jesus. We see him everywhere in the Bible. I know Jesus looked like the Father because he said, 'If you had known Me, you would have known My Father also; from now on you know Him, and have seen Him' (John 14:7). However, he must also have looked like his mother, Mary, so when you look at him, the word of God, you can see human features as well as the divine features. The Bible has a similar mixture of features. We read in the word of God about King Og of Bashan, who had a huge iron bedstead (Deuteronomy 3:11). What is so very important theologically about that, you might say? Not much, perhaps, but it shows that there was something human about the whole

scene. Timothy obviously suffered from indigestion (1 Tim.
5:23). Paul got so fed up with the circumcision party that
he said, 'Oh, I wish they were all emasculated!' (Gal. 5:12).
These details are all very human, not so divine. But the
human and the divine are all wrapped up together into one
as we read the Bible, just as they are in Jesus. It is a good
story. I hope you enjoy reading it just as a story sometimes,
because then, when you see the human touches, if you are
praying it in and into it, this is what will lead you to the
divine.

The Bible is also like a photo album. If you are anything
like Faith and me you will have loads of snapshots of holi-
days, the kids over the years, all thrown haphazardly into a
drawer, until one day you say, 'I'm going to get an album
and stick them all in it.' When we pull the photos out of the
drawer and start looking at them we say, 'Do you remember
this holiday? Remember when the kids were that small?'
Memories are brought back to life. The love that we have
for one another flowers afresh as we remember our shared
history. This is why Jesus told us to remember him in worship at the Lord's table, to meditate day and night. As you
read about the things that Jesus did – when he healed the
leper, when he made friends with fishermen – what he did
is updated and comes alive in the present. As you read the
Bible, you are looking at snapshots, and you are seeing what
Jesus did. You're also seeing where God is going with it all.
As you look between the lines, suddenly, the Lord is
there. You read the information and, suddenly, there is revelation. You see Jesus the word revealed in his word. There
have been times when I have been reading God's word and

the truth of it has been coming in so fast that I have had to say, 'Hold it, it's going too fast, it hurts too much!' That's what revelation feels like sometimes.Isn't this a wonderful book that God has given us? Love God's word.Love anybody who loves God's word through history – whether Jesus himself, Paul, or any man of God, such as John Wesley or Hudson Taylor. We are not going to grow deeply in our prayer life unless we use this wonderful instrument God has given us.We should meditate in his word day and night.It is good to read the word when you get up in the morning.It is good to read the word just before you go to sleep – often it clears out the mind and gets you thinking about the right things.It is like a photo album. It is a parallel to Jesus' incarnation. It is an incomplete play – but it is made complete in Jesus.

When you read Matthew 5:17 you'll see that Jesus came to complete the word: 'Do not think that I came to abolish the Law or the Prophets; I did not come to abolish but to fulfill.' This he does in lots of different ways: he fills it up morally, by coming and living inside us. He fulfils the law by taking all the curses upon his shoulders as he bore our sin in his body on the tree, by completing its history, by fulfilling prophecy. There are so many ways in which Jesus fulfils the Scriptures. He takes them to their destined end, the purpose for which they were given.In him the ceremonial laws of the Old Testament are taken to their end. The Scriptures are very clearly incomplete without Jesus. Incomplete truth is a little bit dangerous. This is why you need to know the story of Jesus.In the Old Testament a Day of Atonement is celebrated every year. But Jesus atones once and for all, so the Day of Atonement is not needed any more. Jesus completes the Scriptures. All Scripture points to Jesus. When we look in his direction then and only then do we fully understand them.

Spiritual growth is about having an encounter and fellowship with God. It is communicating with God. If we only live on dreams and visions and inspiration from time to time, we do not get to grips with God's overall plans and thoughts and ways and how he relates to the universe. We never know how we are meant to relate to each other, how we are meant to relate to him, what the Old Testament really means. If we do not let these testimonies keep bringing knowledge and understanding then we will not be able to worship God with our minds, as Jesus instructs us, we will not understand how to play our part in the play, and we will not be able to contribute to 'hastening the day of the Lord'. We need to soak in his Scriptures, just as Jesus did, just as Paul did, in order that we might understand their testimonies. Praying is the route to soaking!

God sometimes uses the Bible like manna. You probably had some breakfast this morning, but you probably do not remember what you ate! People say to me, 'I went to the meeting, but I can't remember a thing that was said.' This does not matter too much – you have been feeding on the word of God. This is made up of vitamins, carbohydrates and proteins, which all get into your system and give you plenty of energy and power. People who neglect their daily manna will find they have not got a lot of energy to do God's work. They are always too tired or worn out.

If I showed you a picture of Faith and said, 'Look, this is my wife,' you could look at it and say, 'That's not your wife, it's a bit of paper with a picture on it.' But it is a picture of *her*. The Bible is not God, but it is a picture of God. It is not just words – it is *the word*. If you have a picture of your mother standing in a doorway with clematis climbing around the doorframe, you could say, 'This isn't a picture of my mum, it's a picture of some clematis!' The Bible contains the words of God, some words of the devil and some of evil men, but they are all there to set forth the vision and the picture of Jesus, just as the clematis sets off your mother in the picture. There is no problem in calling Jesus the word of God and then calling the Bible the word of God – the Bible is a picture of him. There will be a little bit of clematis around the door!

A friend of mind fell over a cliff when we were quite young. He was not quite a Christian. I had only just become a Christian and I was vigorously trying to convert him when he inconveniently fell over a cliff. I looked down and he moved a bit. I climbed down and the first thing he said to me, sitting up in pain, was, 'Roger, have you got your Bible with you?' So I pulled my little pocket Bible out and gave it to him. He opened it and the first thing he read was 'The Lord sustains all who fall' (Psalm 145:14). He was converted after that. It's a bit like those scriptural calendars. Your aunt sent you one for Christmas and you shoved it in a drawer somewhere and now she is coming to visit. What on earth did you do with it? You rush around trying to find it, you put it up on the wall, and as you flick the last day off and get the calendar up to date, isn't it amazing how the word of God on the calendar for that day speaks to you and guides you with exactly what you needed to hear for your current circumstances and makes concrete what you've been sensing all day?

There are a great many prayers in the Bible over and above the Lord's Prayer. When people say to me they don't know what to pray or how to start praying I always suggest that they read a 'Bible prayer' and start by praying that back to God.

7

Praying in the Breath of God

2 Timothy 3:16 tells us that all Scripture is God-breathed. This is why we should count the Bible as being so precious: it is the breath of God. When you get close to somebody in an intimate relationship and you are so near to that person, face-to-face, that you are just about kissing, that is the place where you can feel the other person's breath. The Bible is the place to go to feel God's breath, to be intimate with him. This verse goes on to break down the different uses of Scripture – teaching, reproof, correction and training in righteousness. The Bible brings us into intimacy with God through the disciplines that we encounter in its pages. As we read the word prayerfully and allow the breath of God's Spirit to seep into us, teaching, reproving, correcting and training, we will find that our lives are full of the discipline that deepens our devotional lives and matures our prayer lives. The nature of Scripture is breath, God's breath, and therefore the only natural way to take it in is to breathe it. We must pray as we read his word!

There are many Christian disciplines to be found in the word of God. Often we only think of the obvious ones – prayer, Bible study – but as we dig deeper we will find many others. They are not rules for us to enforce upon our lifestyles religiously: they are expressions of our desire for greater intimacy with God. When you love someone you work hard at doing the things that bring that person pleasure and you avoid the things that displease him or her. Nobody tells you that you have to act like this, but you know that if you want to stay close to your lover, that is the way to be. This is how we become Christ-like. This is how we start to live in the breath of God. This is how we begin to find that our prayer is no longer shouting into the sky, but rather whispering into the very heart of God. These disciplines open up the heart of God to us.

Secrecy

I want us to think for a minute about our secret lives. We do not often think of secrecy as a Christian discipline. By secrecy, I do not just mean discretion, although it is important not to disclose all kinds of unhelpful information about one another in the body of Christ. Secrecy means not revealing everything that one has in one's heart. See, for example, Matthew 6:3–4, which says that our giving should not be made public. Our left hand should not know what our right is doing. Maybe it applies to receiving a word from the Lord that he does not want you to share with other people. Paul was not permitted by the Lord to tell us the details of his visions in the third heaven or to explain what his 'thorn in the flesh' was in 2 Corinthians 12. The temptation when we find a spiritual grace, whether it is in giving, or revelation, is to tell everybody about it – or at least to tell one or two people. I suppose we feel it sort of boosts our spiritual brownie points somehow! There is a discipline in saying 'I am keeping my giving secret, I am keeping my devotion secret, I am keeping my fasting secret,' and ultimately this matures your relationship with the Lord because you have things in your life that are just between you and God. If you do not have a secret life to your marriage, if you only have a public relationship, then you do not have a real marriage in the end.

There are some people who have no secrets between themselves and God. Their whole spiritual life is laid out for everybody else to see. It is common property. If you have not got any secret things between you and the Lord then the intimacy is very shallow. Of course, sometimes the Lord will encourage you to share what he says to you with others. But there is a time to share and a time to be silent. Remember that Jesus said, 'pray to your Father who is in secret, and your Father who sees what is done in secret will reward you' (Matthew 6:6). He is not saying that every time we pray we must hide in a corner, but rather that we need to have that discipline of a secret life with God. In Revelation 10 John is told not to disclose what God has revealed to him in the seven thunders. This helps to keep us theologians humble – not one of us has a complete eschatology – even if John did!

Spiritual disciplines drawn from Scripture will strengthen our prayer lives. Similarly, we need Scripture to help us to overcome the enemy as he tries to destroy our prayer lives. Prayer is how we commune with God and the devil is constantly trying to put a wedge between that relationship.

Often it is our secret life that comes under attack. James 1:2–4 tells us how to handle these attacks:

> Consider it all joy, my brethren, when you encounter various *trials*, knowing that the testing of your faith produces endurance. And let endurance have its perfect result, so that you may be perfect and complete, lacking in nothing.

James 1:12–16 say:

> Blessed is a man who perseveres *under trial*; for once he has been approved, he will receive the crown of life which the Lord has promised to those who love Him. Let no one say when he is *tempted*, 'I am being *tempted* by God'; for God cannot be tempted by evil, and He Himself does not tempt anyone. But each one is tempted when he is carried away and enticed by his own lust. Then when lust has conceived, it gives birth to sin; and when sin is accomplished, it brings forth death. Do not be deceived, my beloved brethren.

James is talking about trials and temptations that assail our faith. Now, interestingly enough, the Greek for both trial and temptation is the same word. You have to understand from the context whether the text is talking about what we think of as trials – that which come upon us from without to make us stumble – or temptation – something that arises in our own hearts, in that secret place within, to draw us aside into sin. In the end, both have the same effect – they lead us away from God. These verses in James give us a very good explanation of the way temptation works in our lives.

It's a little bit like someone being seduced into a relationship, getting pregnant and giving birth to a baby as a result. Is this not exactly what happens when we sin? There is a *secret* time when temptation first occurs. The seduction, the enticement happens first.

The enemy wants to cause Christians to stumble, so he runs through his list of possible vices and hits upon, let's say, bitterness and unforgiveness. He needs to tempt you to be unforgiving. So what does he do? Well, first of all he starts to draw you aside.He starts on you when you are alone, in private. The most hidden and private part of a person is, of course, the mind – we need to remember that temptation starts in the battleground of the mind. He identifies the offence you felt when you were treated badly and he begins to feed it. He causes you to dwell upon the incident. He helps you to compare the other person's conduct with your impeccable behaviour. You would never do such a thing! And before you know it, you are angrier than you were to start with. The offence now seems unforgivable and the person outrageous for perpetrating it. The next time you see the person you have built up such a horrendous picture of the crime in your mind that you act rudely, angrily and dismissively towards him or her. The gulf widens and bitterness and unforgiveness set in.

There are countless examples of this process. We all know it is very true in the area of sexual temptations. The temptation to be unfaithful to your spouse begins long before you are ever in a situation to act upon your immoral desire. It begins with wrong thoughts about that other person in the imagination. This is the enemy's seduction. If you give place to it and you start to entertain that thought then a conception of sin occurs. It is all in secret at first – no one else knows about it. But very soon it starts to grow within you, like a pregnancy, and it is not long before the secret becomes evident to other people. James says that eventually the temptation, when it has been conceived, will give birth to sin, and that sin when it is fully grown gives birth to death. It is a horrific picture of the child that is growing within eventually emerging and instead of being life, as a normal child would be, being death. Sin brings death to your spiritual life. James is warning us that we need discipline in our secret life, and if we do not share the hidden places of our hearts with the Lord in prayer, the enemy will take that place in our lives and begin his seductions. Fill your imagination with the secret intimacy of communion with Christ and you will be drawn into the Holy of Holies of God's presence. That is the place to receive God's gift so that we can defeat the enemy and his temptations.

Overcoming

> Every good thing given and every perfect gift is from above, coming down from the Father of lights, with whom there is no variation or shifting shadow. In the exercise of His will He brought us forth by the word of truth, so that we would be a kind of first fruits among His creatures (James 1:17–18).

James is encouraging us here that it is not all bad news! As opposed to sin and the enemy at work, the Spirit is also

active in us, conceiving the work of God in us, giving birth
to life so that we become the first fruits of his creation. So
why is it that the work of the enemy always seems to be so
much stronger and more powerful? Romans 5 – 7 show us
three ways that sin comes to lead us astray. In Romans 6:12
Paul says, 'do not let sin reign in your mortal body'. Sin is a
king. Sin comes demanding obedience, and we know that
some temptation feels just like that. You can be almost
overwhelmed by the temptation at times. This is because we
were made for obedience. Of course, that is intended to be
obedience to God, for we are his creatures, but it also means
we are prone to obey Satan when he too comes like a king.
Sometimes people describe their sin as coming over them
like a huge wave. When we feel that temptation overwhelm
us, Paul says, 'Do not let sin reign!' We have to recognise that
the enemy is really determined to try to knock us off our
feet. Sometimes he will do it when we are unaware, because
obviously it is easier to knock people off their feet if they
are not expecting the blow. Let us recognise that sometimes
sin comes upon us like that. We also need to be prepared to
restore others when that happens to them. You will remember that Paul says, 'Brethren, even if anyone is caught in any
trespass, you who are spiritual, restore such a one in a spirit
of gentleness; each one looking to yourself, so that you too
will not be tempted' (Galatians 6:1). It is foolhardy to try
and help another and ignore that the same temptation, or
even another, might come at us – for example, our own
pride. Then, if you do fall, you may feel that you are not
strong enough to stand up again, but you can instantly
repent, and that will help you not to fall again. The big

danger is that once the enemy has knocked you over you think, 'Well, I may as well stay here now!' and you continue in the sin. Don't let sin rule over you – let Jesus be your Lord!

Paul also presents sin and temptation as an *employer*. In Romans 6:23 he says, 'For the wages of sin is death, but the free gift of God is eternal life in Christ Jesus our Lord.' Wages are what you get paid. You look forward to receiving them once a week or month. The great deception of Satan is to tell you that the wages will be good: this is how he is able to tempt us, like an employer. 'If you give place to sin in this area, you will get this back. You will feel better here. You will be rewarded there. You will get that extra sense of wellbeing – these are the perks!' If there were no perks to be gained from sinning then you probably wouldn't sin at all, would you? But the payback ultimately is death. Just as James explains that the child produced is death, so Paul says the wages of sin are ultimately death: spiritual and physical, according to Genesis 2 and 3.

Finally, Paul talks about sin and temptation coming to us like a husband to a wife (Roman 7:2–6). A married woman is bound by law to a husband for as long as he lives, but if her husband dies, she is discharged from the law concerning the husband.[3] How is sin like your husband? When you are married you have an identity. You belong to the other person. So what the enemy will often do is say to you, 'You really belong

---

[3] Many commentators will suggest that in this analogy Paul has changed the subject of his first two images to see the husband not as sin but as the Law. However, I suggest that it is better to be consistent. The marriage certificate is the Law and the husband is a third picture of sin.

to sin! You don't really belong to all this spiritual stuff, you don't belong to all this godliness and holiness, you belong to sin!' We start to believe that this is our identity. And if we belong there, we had better start behaving suitably. The enemy will often deceive us by the way he portrays who we are. He tells us that we really belong to him.

I remember a man who was very, very tempted. He had a very broken background, a history of immorality, a lot of pressure and a lot of twistedness. He was trying to get his life sorted out, but he was struggling with overwhelming temptations in his mind. One day, as we were praying for him, I said to him: 'When you look into your own heart, what sort of a person do you see?'

'I see this ugly, twisted, corrupt person looking back at me,' he said.

'That is the lie of the Devil,' I responded. 'That is what we need to change, because you have been made a new creature through Christ, and there is a new life within you. We need to break the power of that wrong image of your-self so that you see yourself as someone born again in Christ with a new life and a power to live for God.'

We prayed in that way and God really helped that man move forward with him. It was a very crucial point in the whole pilgrimage that he was on, to recognise that he was a new creature in Christ. We are no longer bound to sin. Paul says that through Christ's death sin has died and we are free to be joined to Christ. Through Christ's death we are legally separated from that old relation-ship with sin and have a right to a new relationship with God.

Joy

We have looked at some of the strategies that the enemy employs to draw us away from communion with God. If we do not look to Scripture to understand them we will always be caught off guard. Our secret lives, our prayer lives, will get overrun with all sorts of other things and we will no longer be in the place where we can feel the intimacy of God's breath on our face. So let us turn to Scripture for the antidote to the enemy's strategy. James chapter 1 mentions joy. Cultivate joy. If we can cultivate joy in our hearts day by day this is an antidote to some of the poisonous words that the enemy sows in. A lot of his poison rides in on the waves of depression we feel as we think about our trials and temptations. But if we can cultivate a heart of joy by worshipping, praising and loving the Lord, lifting up our hearts to him, that will help us to keep steady under pressure. Try and get used to singing (even if you are tone deaf!) – it is hard to stay sad when you have a song on your lips. Try it! Sometimes, when there is real pressure on you, if you can start praising God you will push the enemy away. Believe me, I have done this over and over, so I know that this is true!

Another way to combat depression and make sure that the enemy cannot divert you from God's purposes is through distraction. When our minds start to become one-track, only thinking about the awful trials we are facing at the moment, only considering the awful thing we are tempted to do, we need to distract ourselves by dwelling on more productive things. Do something positive to serve somebody else. Or maybe just do something really practical – go and make an omelette, write a letter or something! Sometimes we need wisdom to distract ourselves from our troubles. Distraction is not repression. Repression will actually push problems down deeper inside and end up lodging them more securely. Distraction diverts you to think on whatever things are good, pure, honest, lovely and of good report. Such reflection brings faith that God will rescue you from trials and temptations. He has said that he will not allow you to be tempted beyond what you can bear. He has promised that there will always be a way out of temptation. That means that if we give way while knowing that promise, we have actually chosen, to some degree, to give way – we didn't have to. On one level that may seem condemning (although we have all been there), but on another level it is incredibly empowering. There is a way out. We do not have to choose wrongly. We can, with God's help, master the sin crouching at our door (Gen. 4:7).

One of my heroes is John Wesley. It is said of him that he never remembered being depressed for longer than fifteen minutes when he was attacked in this way. That is rather remarkable for a man who had a difficult marriage. This man must have been disciplined in dealing with pressures. Psalm 42 is one of my favourite psalms for dealing with depression and oppression in life. It moves beautifully between prayer, lament and exhortation to the soul. This psalm became very precious to me when our son was diagnosed with cancer and we were under pressure, of course, as a family. It is a long and involved story, but we had an exciting breakthrough in prayer when at a certain point we felt that God had stepped in. The doctors had given our son twelve weeks to live, but we knew we had this new peace in our hearts. When they took further X-rays all the cancer lumps had gone – they had been in his neck, arm, lungs, spleen and stomach. But we were still waiting for the final lumbar puncture test on his central nervous system and brain to find whether any cancer growth was still there. So we had a little ray of hope, but the prognosis was still very serious. I had been away at a conference but was travelling back to London to go to the hospital and get the results. Very early in the morning, I opened up my daily Bible reading, which for that day was Psalm 42. Verse 5 says: 'Why are you in despair, O my soul? And why have you become disturbed within me? Hope in God, for I shall again praise Him for the help of His presence.' I said to myself that early Monday morning, 'I'm not depressed, we've seen a terrific breakthrough!' And I read on and got to verse 11: 'Why are you in despair, O my soul? And why have you become disturbed within me? Hope in God, for I shall yet praise Him, the help of my countenance and my God.' Then again, I read in Psalm 43:5: 'Why are you in despair, O my soul? And why are you disturbed within me? Hope in God, for I shall again praise Him, the help of my countenance and my God.' I was perplexed! I wasn't feeling down, I was quite encouraged! But as I read those words it began to dawn on me that God was trying to say something to me. I was being pretty slow and it took the Lord three tries to get it through, but I realised that there was a chance that a challenge was ahead, and it could make me depressed. When I got to the hospital the consultant said that the results of the lumbar puncture test were much the same as before. It could have taken the wind out of my sails after the exaltation of believing that God had broken in and healed my son. But the Lord had prepared me for this news and in one sense I was not surprised at what the consultant said to me. For a further three months we understood from the medical point of view that my son still had cancer hidden away in his spinal fluid, although all lumps in the other five places had disappeared. We found out later that the results of the test had actually been clear, but the doctors couldn't believe that all those cells had just disappeared from my son's body, and they didn't want to give us false hope. Our son was fully healed! But for those three months we had to try and find peace in the face of the medical declaration that our son was dying. There were times when I prayed and poured out my heart to the Lord; there were times when I could not pray, exactly, but I lamented and got rid of my unbelief that way; and there were times when I told myself off. 'Why are you in despair, O my soul?' Through it all, the peace I felt was incredible. I remember saying to myself 'If you were a better father you'd be much more worried.' But God was using this Psalm to empower my prayers and help me find faith in them.

How did the psalmist break through his trials and temptations and find freedom from depression?

Firstly, he uses reason: 'Why are you cast down?' 'Why has this happened?' (verse 5). 'Why do I go mourning because of the oppression of the enemy?' (verse 9). Sometimes we need to ask questions, to think, and try to understand what is happening to us. If we just give in to depression and give up thinking about it we are never going to beat it. We should be asking God to illuminate our mind, because he does have answers. Six times in these two Psalms (42 and 43) the psalmist asks 'Why?' God intends us to ask why. Jesus did on the cross: 'Why have you forsaken me?' The answer is in Psalm 22: 'Yet You are holy ...But I am a worm and not a man, a reproach of men and despised by the people' (verses 2–6). Jesus got an answer because he asked the questions, and we are meant to ask questions in such times.

Secondly, he uses his memory. Psalm 42:4 says: 'These things I remember and I pour out my soul ...' and verse 6: 'Therefore I remember You from the land ...' We are told to take communion in remembrance of Jesus and the wonderful things that God has done. When I feel sorry for myself and give way to depression I only need to think back to how God healed my son, or the wonder that he gave me such a super wife, or the terrific experiences we have had of seeing many people converted, and I start to feel better. When we look back it gives us courage to look forward and face the future and believe that God can do something good in our present situation too. That is why the psalmist bursts out in faith in Psalm 43:3: 'O send out Your light and Your truth, let them lead me; let them bring me to Your holy hill ...'

Thirdly, he talks to himself! 'Soul why are you cast down?' Do you speak to yourself? It's not crazy – it's a very healthy thing to do! You get your soul by the scruff of the neck and you start shaking it: 'Soul, why are you cast down?' Slap, slap, slap! And the soul says, 'Don't hit me, don't hit me again, I feel sorry for myself.' And you say, 'Soul, cheer up!'

Your soul replies, 'Leave me alone, leave me alone!' When you are sinking into a dark depression, talk to your soul and tell it to start rejoicing, and the light comes out again. In Psalm 42:5 the psalmist says, 'praise *Him* for the help of *His* face/presence', but in verse 11 he says, 'the help of *my* countenance and *my* God'. If you look into the face of God for a while, your face begins to shine, just as Moses came down from the mountain with his face shining after communing with God. Instead of looking dark and dismal, we can shine through our trials!

Finally, he prays aloud. You will notice that in Psalm 42:8–9 he says 'a prayer to the God of my life. I will say to God my rock ...' Sometimes just praying isn't enough, we need to speak out our prayers, declare them, not just dream them inside. It is easy to fall asleep when you pray inside your head. But as you pray aloud, you begin to be aware that God is listening, and this brings faith that he might actually do something!

The Bible can help us to pray. It can help us better to understand the problems we are praying about. It can also show us practically how to overcome the enemy when he tries to drive us away from prayer using trials and temptations.

Assimilation

Perhaps one of the most stimulating ways in which the God-breathed Bible can help us to pray is through what I call 'assimilation'. This is a very deep concept, but very wonderful! As we live in the Bible day by day, we will find prayers there that we can take up and use to help us to pray. However, we can go even further than that, until we slip into the very bloodstream of God's life, and are assimilated into its truths and purposes as we are saturated by its contents. There are great similarities between Daniel and Zacharias, John the Baptist's father. Perhaps Zacharias had saturated himself in the book of Daniel and been assimilated into the life and purposes of God by its pages. The most obvious similarity is that both men were visited by Gabriel. Both also had their encounter at the time of the evening sacrifice, the time of offering incense (Luke 1:10; Daniel 9:20). Both men were afraid (Luke 1:12; Daniel 8:17, 10:7). Both had visions (Luke 1:22; Daniel 9 and 10). Both were struck dumb as a result (Luke 1:22; Daniel 10:15). Wisdom and righteousness are combined themes in both stories (Luke 1:17 – in the Greek, Daniel 12:3). This is an unusual and therefore distinctive combination of two concepts in Scripture. Finally, for Daniel, Jeremiah's prophecy of seventy years to the end time (eschaton) becomes four hundred and ninety years (seventy times seven). Luke's story records four hundred and ninety days starting from John the Baptist's conception until the day when Jesus was presented in the Temple and the new end-time era of the Messiah dawned (Luke 2:21–22; Daniel 9:24).

I have no doubt that Zacharias and Elizabeth had ceased praying for a child long before the vision came to Zacharias. But God had not forgotten their prayers. So as Zacharias offered incense to the Lord and the people prayed for the redemption of Israel, God answered their assimilated prayers. The prayers of the people joined with the cries for freedom from oppression offered through Israel's history since Daniel's prophecy, and merged with Zacharias' personal and domestic prayers for a son to bring forth a glorious answer in John the Baptist – the forerunner for Christ, the subject of Daniel's prophecy.

Living in the breath of God and breathing in Scripture will enhance both our prayers and our response to God and assimilate them into his purposes for us and the world.

8

Pressures in Prayer

We have thought in the previous chapter about the power of Scripture in our prayers to overcome the enemy. Prayer is often difficult because it is so powerful in defeating the enemy. It is our primary weapon against him and thus he does all he can to disable us from praying. That is why prayer is such hard work sometimes – we are fighting a battle with the devil.

The whole world really does lie in the hand of the enemy (1 John 5:19). We are in the business of fighting and punching into enemy lines with our prayers. I know that this is the day the Lord made, I know that this is God's earth ultimately, but the enemy has got a grip on it. There is a 'supernatural envelope' around the earth that tries to contain us, hold us in, and make us feel that our prayers can't get anywhere. In the final analysis all the trials that come upon us have the energy of the enemy behind them. Jesus heals a woman who has been physically bound with back problems for eighteen years. The Bible tells us she was bound by Satan (Luke 13:10–17). Today we might be able to perform corrective surgery, we might think back problems are just part of the human condition, and that may be so, but wherever there is pressure it comes ultimately from the energy and the pressure of Satan. We need to recognise that we are in a war and therefore we have to deal with these pressures aggressively.

The way the enemy works is to pressurise us until we lose our faith in prayer and stop praying altogether. I want us to think about 1 Samuel 30 for a little bit. It tells the story of David after he had been anointed by Samuel but had not yet come to the throne. He was living in the wilderness and trying to be at peace with the Philistines, therefore he was required to go to war alongside the Philistine king. But other Philistine lords were unhappy having Israelites on their side because they feared that their allegiance was false, so David and his men were sent back to their camp at Ziklag. When they arrived they found that the Amalekites, another enemy, had raided their encampment, burned it down and carried off all the women and children. David found that in his absence everything had been stolen from him. Sometimes we can feel as though the enemy has robbed us of everything. It is as though he has simply walked into your life and just helped himself to whatever he wanted. It is an absolutely devastating feeling. At that point you can either say, 'Right, I'm just going to give up!' and allow the enemy to replace all your faith with bitterness, disappointment and resistance towards God (and in that place prayer is practically impossible), or you can follow David's example.

First of all, David and his men 'lifted their voices and wept until there was no strength in them to weep'. This may not sound very productive, but the reason they wept was because they were facing their sorrow and grieving appropriately. Some people try to be spiritual in a crisis by putting on a brave face and refusing to accept that anything is wrong, even adding that it must be God's will. All this does is contain the grief and anger and allow it to fester until it comes out at some later point, often when it is least expected or appropriate. If things have gone horribly wrong in some area we need to face it, and if necessary we need to accept responsibility and discipline for it, if our own sin contributed to the circumstances. David was blamed by the people for not protecting them properly and leaving them vulnerable, and because of this we are told he was greatly distressed. Not only was he sorry for the loss of his own wives, but he had to carry the responsibility for his people's losses too. Grief and repentance often go hand in hand, but this is a healthy first response to the devastation of the enemy in our lives.

However, David did not remain in that place of grief. What he did next was to '[strengthen] himself in the Lord his God'. How do we do this? We can get rid of our guilt by receiving forgiveness from the Lord. Repentance does not mean we have to beat ourselves up about something forever – we can be restored in his forgiveness and move on. But perhaps you feel that the situation is really the result of somebody else's sin or negligence. In that case we need to release forgiveness, just as we were talking about in the outline of the Lord's Prayer. It might seem hard to forgive others when their actions leave you feeling robbed and floored by the enemy, especially when they are not affected at all. But remember Jesus on the cross: 'Father, forgive them; for they do not know what they are doing' (Luke 23:34).

Sometimes the enemy uses people to destroy your faith and happiness through the bitterness you feel toward them for their mistakes. They may not even be aware of what they have done; they may have been manipulated by the devil into hurting you, and would never have done it intentionally. Another person's sins against you are never directly aimed at you. It is just that person's flesh, that person being just plain awkward, difficult and unpleasant – human beings can be like that. The enemy made use of the person to bring you down. When we receive and release forgiveness for a situation we begin to allow the grief to process. We are no longer overwhelmed by the horror of it all, our own mistakes, other people's, but we can see things in perspective and are ready to receive God's mind on it all.

Finally, David enquired of the Lord as to what he should do. Often when we find it hard to hear God in a crisis it is because we have not yet gone through the first two steps that David took. It is no good trying to hear God's answer to something if we are still struggling with why it had to happen, whose fault it was and how devastated we feel. Once we have accepted the problem, grieved and strengthened ourselves, then we are ready to hear God's instruction and obey. Maybe there is something the Lord wants us to do that will address things. We should ask him, as David did, 'How should I go forward from this point, Lord? Is there something I need to set in place in my life so that I am not vulnerable in that area again? Is there some action I can take to put things back to the way they were and gain back the ground from the enemy? What do you want me to do?' There is an old prayer that says: 'Lord, give me the grace to accept the things I cannot change. Give me the faith to change the things that can be changed. Give me the wisdom to know the difference.' This is a very valuable prayer. Some things that go wrong cannot be changed outwardly. Some losses can never be restored. Although, having said this, God can wonderfully redeem the past. Things may not all go back to the way they were as if nothing had ever happened, but things can be transformed so that the event becomes a place not of horror and pain but a place where the grace of God was found. That is the message of the cross, of course. The darkest and most painful events can be the means of salvation and grace to be released.

Of course, some things can be changed and put back together again, if only we have the courage and the faith to do things differently. Relationships may break down and become damaged and it may seem as if they can never be healed, but with God's help we can start to act differently. Even where we thought love was lost and irretrievable God can show us how to find it again and 'dead' relationships can be resurrected. The enemy will try to pour despair into you and tell you that things cannot improve. We need to learn to pray: 'Lord, I release to you the things that I cannot change now. Restore to me my joy, my peace, my faith, my courage so that I can change the things that can be put right and move on.' Sometimes when we have been knocked down by the enemy we don't feel able to pick ourselves up and start again. We don't want to come before God in prayer and hear his solutions because we are tired and disheartened. The enemy will put pressure on us in all sorts of different ways to keep us from the Lord. He will use physical pressures.

If you have bad digestion, for instance, it may seem trivial but you are a very disadvantaged person. You could be tempted to feel sorry for yourself all the time. People who have good digestion can afford to be sanguine and bounce around the place, but you have to walk around, miserable and melancholic, with your stomach grinding away. You will be prone to depression. You will feel at a disadvantage to other Christians: 'Nobody else has to cope with this sort of pain!' The enemy will drop this sort of thing into your mind all the time. The encouraging thing is that our body, our physical condition, has cycles. Sometimes our body is on top form and other times it is going through a rough patch. If your body is in pain, every little wobble in life will seem a lot worse. If you are feeling suicidal, remember that tomorrow morning you may feel a lot better. As the discomfort in your body starts to ease, the stress and depression also lift, because the cycle of physical condition has gone around full circle. And so with that knowledge you can look forward to and begin to anticipate God's intervention into the things that are getting you down.

The enemy will bring emotional pressures to floor you. Sorrow, grief and bereavement occur in life and can rob people of their faith. This is often because they do not understand sorrow and the grieving process, and they do not know that things will not always feel like this – they will get better. Separation brings sorrow. Our younger daughter used to weep night after night when her sister, nine years older, left home for university. It was no good saying to her 'You mustn't cry' – she was depressed. Circumstances can bring that kind of depression into our lives. But it doesn't last forever. If we treat depressed people as though they will never get through it, we give in to depression, we allow it to overcome us and rule us. We have got to learn the disciplines of how to cope with sorrow so that we do not become paralysed and useless for God. Francis of Assisi commanded his friars to be as happy as they possibly could. It was a part of their spiritual discipline, and it should be a part of ours, so that we do not inflict our miseries on everyone else. Sorrow may last for a night but joy comes in the morning. We will grieve, but we will get through it, and the Lord will heal our hearts and help us to move on.

The enemy will also use mental pressures. Our lives can get so busy and we move so quickly from one thing to the next that our minds get full of all the things we are supposed to be doing, leaving no room for the peace of Christ. In these times problems can become irrationally overwhelming. Satan uses fear and panic that we are going to lose our minds and drop all the balls we are juggling. Instead of being driven to God we are driven away. Fear produces unbelief and unbelief stifles prayer. Instead of allowing these things to overwhelm our minds we must pray for peace and ask God to put our responsibilities and priorities into perspective. The things we fear are never so bad as we think they might be, especially as we cover them all in prayer. 'Be anxious for nothing, but in everything by prayer and supplication with thanksgiving let your requests be made known to God. And the peace of God, which surpasses all comprehension, will guard your hearts and your minds in Christ Jesus' (Philippians 4:6–7).

Finally, there are spiritual pressures from the devil. I have already indicated that he is behind all these pressures. He is trying to make use of them to keep you down and stop you praying, so that you are unable to get up and do something for God. All pressure comes ultimately from the devil, but at times he will make a direct impact on us. You do not know why you feel as you do. You do not know why you are being pushed down inwardly. The source is satanic. You might walk into a room where spiritualism has been taking place, for example, and you immediately stop breathing spiritually. Just as when you walk into a room full of gas and you stop breathing, if there is the presence of something supernaturally negative and dark, you just hold back, you react. Satan puts direct pressure on your spirit. Not just thoughts into the mind, not just by whispering discouragement into your emotions, not any obvious outward or physical cause, but you can suddenly feel the presence of negativism, darkness and despair. That is the enemy trying to stop you being useful to God. Anyone who has been engaged in spiritual warfare and intercession will know at times you want to pray, you know you ought to pray, but there is such a pressure on you saying 'You dare not go into this room, do not keep praying over this thing.' That is the enemy bringing fear and oppression. Do not feel that you are being unspiritual. Remember Gesthemane and the three places in John's Gospel (11:33, 12:27, 13:21) when Jesus says that he is 'deeply moved in spirit', that his 'soul has become troubled', and that he is 'troubled in spirit'. Now, of course, there was nothing in Jesus that gave room to Satan at all. 'The ruler of the world is coming, and he has nothing in Me' (John 14:30). It was not sin that made Jesus feel like that, simply that the general atmosphere of the darkness was descending on him with all its ability to bring horror. 'But this hour and the power of darkness are yours' Jesus said to his enemies (Luke 22:53). Remember, in those moments of absolute gloom and despair, it is the enemy! You can get up and shout him out! Tell him to get off your back. If you mean business, you can attack the enemy and say, 'Out, in Jesus' name!' It is remarkable how the sun breaks through. You begin to see light in your soul. Unbelief is a cause of spiritual depression. We all know that we are believers, but some of us do not believe very much. We all want to be bigger in faith and confidence, and obviously a part of our spiritual growth is to persevere in prayer, under pressure, believing that we are doing some good somewhere along the line, even if we can't see anything at present.

When Samson wanted a riddle for the Philistines he remembered how a young lion had come roaring out from the vineyard to destroy him. With his own bare hands he had grabbed hold of the lion and killed it. Samson was a person to whom God had given extraordinary boldness and strength. He had flung the dead carcass aside and told nobody of what he had done. But when he next passed that way he noticed that in the lion's carcass there was a swarm of bees making honey, so he took the honey and ate it. Remembering this event, he created this riddle for the Philistines: 'Out of the eater came something to eat, and out of the strong came something sweet' (Judges 14:14). It is worth learning this riddle – you can say it to yourself when you feel that the enemy has really overcome you and destroyed you. Maybe you have fallen in some area of temptation, or maybe a trial is overwhelming you. You can say to yourself again: 'Out of the eater came something to eat, and out of the strong came something sweet.' That very tempta- tion that would try to eat you up can strengthen you as you learn to overcome. A dear friend of ours who is now with the Lord and who had a great many trials in her life used to say: 'Trials make some people bitter, and other people better.' She had really proved in her life that she was some- body sweeter for trials.

I have a little proverb for us. Did you know that you can find cricket in the Bible? Well, one of my favourite 'cricket' verses is in Ephesians 5:16, which says, 'making the most of (redeeming) your time, because the days are evil'. Now, each evil day is like a cricket ball bowled at you. It is an evil ball because the enemy bowled it. It is coming at you to get you out. Each evil day comes from the hand of the enemy, but if you play it right you can score with it! You redeem an evil ball and it becomes a good ball. We do this by recognising the pressures, temptations and trials, the 'googlies' the enemy throws at us, and hitting them for six in prayer. And each day we score, we are notching up runs for Jesus.

9

Passionate Prayer

In this chapter I wish to isolate two elements of prayer – supplication and intercession – and one element of praise – high praise. When we make supplication and intercede we are bordering on what we call 'spiritual warfare', the kind of prayer that sees God's will done 'on earth as it is in heaven' (Matthew 6:10). We are wrestling 'not against flesh and blood, but against the rulers, against the powers, against the world forces of this darkness, against the spiritual forces of wickedness in the heavenly places' (Ephesians 6:12). We must come into the battle charged up with love through worship, filled with power through thanksgiving, and with energy to see things change! Energy is necessary in prayer. It is said of Elijah that he prayed fervently because he was 'praying in his prayer' (James 5:17). It is almost as though he was giving birth to what he was praying for. Sometimes when we are praying we are not praying our prayer into being. But that is what the Greek text of James says we must do – we must 'pray in' our prayers. Again, some of us when we pray are too relaxed, too 'laid back' – our intercession is lacking in energy and we do not put nearly enough into it! Jesus prayed with such energy and such emotion that drops of blood appeared on his forehead. That is supplication! That is intercession! If this is how the Son of God prayed it will not be surprising if at times we too are going to pray with groanings that cannot be articulated.

Let us look at the priority of comprehensive prayer. 1 Timothy 2:1 says 'First of all, then, I urge that entreaties and prayers, petitions and thanksgivings, be made on behalf of all ...' Paul does not tell Timothy to preach the gospel first of all, nor does he say love your neighbour first of all. No, he says – you must pray first of all.

When we pray with energy, fervour and emotion, putting everything we have into our intercession, that is in itself an appeal to God. We do not cast out demons by politely asking them to 'Please move over and leave' – demons will not respond to that! We say rather 'Out! In the name of Jesus!' – we put some energy into it! So too when it comes to supplication and intercession we are talking about *passion*.

Firstly, Paul says, 'I urge that entreaties and prayers, petitions and thanksgivings, be made on behalf of all ...' There are four types of prayer, for all people. It is relatively easy to pray for all people, but it is not always so easy to pray for them with all types of prayer, for instance, thanksgiving!

Secondly, Paul decides to pray for kings. It is, of course, very important to pray for people who are in high places and who have responsible positions in the scheme of things, but the kind of prayer that Paul urges is first for the ordinary people all around us – our neighbours, colleagues and friends. It is right to pray regularly for the queen and her ministers, for when we pray for those in authority we are praying for those who can shut or open doors on behalf of God. They do not necessarily do this willingly, but they are the keys that God can turn. There is a verse in Proverbs that says 'The king's heart is like channels of water in the hand of the Lord; He turns it wherever He wishes' (Proverbs 21:1). Paul, then, enjoins us to pray 'for kings and all who are in authority, so that we may lead a tranquil and quiet life in all godliness and dignity. This is good and acceptable in the sight of God our Savior' (1 Timothy 2:2–3). Why does it please him? Because he 'desires all men to be saved and to come to the knowledge of the truth. For there is one God, and one mediator also between God and men, the man Christ Jesus, who gave Himself as a ransom for all' (1 Timothy 2:4–6). These verses from Paul's letter to Timothy refute the argument (sometimes heard in Western Christian circles) that 'we shouldn't pray for everybody'; the attitude that says 'Well, they're all going to be saved anyway because God has already chosen who's going to heaven and it won't make any difference whether you pray or whether you don't!' We often meet this attitude in our European culture and it is easy to inherit it as complacency and lack of passion in prayer. God our Saviour 'desires *all* men to be saved and to come to the knowledge of the truth. For ... Christ Jesus ... gave Himself as a ransom for *all*.' Not for some. Not for one or two. For all! So pray for all, and pray that they may be converted.

As we pray for all men we pray also for peaceful and quiet lives to enable us to spread the gospel better, for we know that the more the gospel advances and the more we move into the end time the more pressure comes back the other way. We can see that happening as we push forward and people are saved. At the same time a 'stirring up' takes place.

All over the world there are more wars every year and this escalation in hostility corresponds with the advance of the gospel. So pray for peace so that when we come to the last great push and the coming of the millennium there will be a thousand years of peace!

'Intercession' is a word that causes difficulties for some people. It means to 'meet with', to 'come between', even 'to come against' or 'to intervene'. In Romans 11 we have a good example of the 'come against' meaning. In verse 2 Paul says, 'God has not rejected His people whom He foreknew. Or do you not know what the Scripture says in the passage about Elijah, how he *pleads* with God *against* Israel?' We do not suggest that you spend too much time praying against people, but it is worth noting that this kind of praying (which is intercessory praying) does meet opposition. There is a third party clearly in view in this kind of praying, and it is the aggressive aspect that distinguishes this type of prayer, although you cannot completely separate it from the others. There are times when we come before the Lord in supplication and within minutes we are resisting or 'coming against' something on the horizontal, and before we know it we are interceding. Prayer moves from one kind to another as easily as that, so much so that Jesus says: 'whoever says to this mountain, "Be taken up and cast into the sea," and does not doubt in his heart, but believes that what he says is going to happen, it will be granted him. Therefore I say to you, all things for which you pray and ask, believe that you have received them, and they will be granted you' (Mark 11:23–24). We have already seen that Jesus calls this prayer, even though we are speaking horizontally, because it is done in his presence. In intercession we met a resistance and an unbelief that can only be overcome in the presence of the Lord.

Let us return to the teaching of our Lord beginning in Luke 22:41:

The prayer of Jesus in the garden of Gethsemane was within the context of temptation – the enemy was there too. Jesus teaches us to pray 'do not lead us into temptation, but deliver us from [the evil one]' (Matthew 6:13). We see that in our circumstances in a fallen world temptation is always there. It surrounds us and we need God's help not to enter it or fall in accidentally. Moreover, the enemy especially sits up and takes notice when we pray! Jesus prayed in the atmosphere and the vicinity of temptation and it cost him an attack by the devil, who oppressed him with fear of what it would mean to go to the cross. Jesus, who had never been out of his father's bosom throughout eternity, was faced with the alienation of the cross. He had to break through the pressure of the enemy to be able to pray 'yet not My will, but Yours be done' (Luke 22:42). The enemy must have had a suspicion that when Jesus got up from his knees after praying he, Satan, was finished! Satan, in his arrogance, would be brought into mockery as Jesus brought principalities and powers, might and dominion, into the chains of the triumph of Calvary (Colossians 2:14,15). It was not at the resurrection but on the cross that Jesus demonstrated that every power had been put under his feet. Jesus did not go from Gethsemane to the cross as a victim but marched there as a victor. The battle had already been fought and won in Jesus. In Gethsemane there was supplication and intercession beyond anything that we

could ever know as Christ prayed both vertically and horizontally and under great pressure from the enemy.

Intercession and the prophets

I want to pick out a few points from Zechariah.

1. In Zechariah 12:11–14 the prophet talks of a time of distress
   and mourning. There is a place for mourning in intercession
   and spiritual warfare. Mourning and fasting are closely
   related[4] – both are means of discovering real power in our
   prayer. When we have seen into the heart of Jesus and
   realised how big his desires are it is then that we realise we
   need more spiritual power to start to do something about it!

2. The result is Zechariah 13:1–2:

   In that day a fountain will be opened for the house of David
   and for the inhabitants of Jerusalem, for sin and for impurity.
   'It will come about in that day,' declares the Lord of hosts, 'that
   I will cut off the names of the idols from the land, and they
   will no longer be remembered; and I will also remove the
   prophets and the unclean spirit from the land.'

   This is the only place in the Old Testament where an
   unclean spirit is mentioned, and it is in the context of
   impurity and uncleanness amongst Israel. But as they

---

[4] See 'Fasting' by Roger Forster (Sovereign World).

pray, mourn and fast a fountain opens up, and is made available to cleanse that impurity and for God to remove every false prophet and every unclean spirit. False prophets and unclean spirits go together because it is a prophet who brings a spirit. If he is a prophet of the Lord he brings the Holy Spirit. If he is a false prophet he brings an unclean spirit. In order to cleanse the land we need the washing flow of the fountain that has been opened up through the cross. It is the prayers of repentant people who have seen the heart of God and mourned with him for the uncleanness of the world who release the cleansing power of forgiveness from the cross.

3. When the Holy Spirit began to clean out all the false prophets (and there must have been a lot of them) people were afraid to reveal their own spirit to others.

Also it will come about in that day that the prophets will each be ashamed of his vision when he prophesies, and they will not put on a hairy robe in order to deceive; but he will say, 'I am not a prophet; I am a tiller of the ground, for a man sold me as a slave in my youth' (Zechariah 13:4–5).

Everyone was so afraid of being found false and of being killed that even those who might have been true prophets hid away!

This still happens today. In the middle of a great spate of prophecies, some of them will be ludicrous, wild and bizarre, and so we begin to despise prophets. In 1 Thessalonians 5:19–20 Paul says, 'Do not quench the Spirit; do not despise prophetic utterances.'It is when we begin to despise prophecy that a danger arises because everybody becomes afraid to speak out what is in their spirit. This is an overreaction that allows the enemy to ensure that prophesies cease. It was the prophetic word that opened up the understanding of the cross and its cleansing fountains in the first place. But now the prophets are afraid to be prophets because so many have been purged and found to be false. So the true prophets do not show themselves or allow themselves to be known as prophets at all.

4. One of the strangest verses (with many different interpretations) is found in Zechariah 13:6: 'And one will say to him, "What are these wounds between your arms?" Then he will say, "Those with which I was wounded in the house of my friends."'

There are many ways of understanding these very deep verses. However, one very poignant thing is that these prophets, who could be releasing God's word to others, are being treated in the same way as Jesus, who was pierced being charged as a false prophet. Just as prayer is not only vertical between you and God, but can also be horizontal, so prophecy is both horizontal and vertical. It is horizontal as we prophesy to others what God places on our hearts to release God's grace to them, but it is also vertical when God uses us as pictures and reflections of what is going on in his own heart and will. So here the prophet's body is experiencing what Jesus would experience years later as his own people wounded him and challenged his prophetic authority. The prophetic ministry is under pressure today because it tends to be downgraded, misunderstood and misused. We limit it, saying 'God only speaks in this way or that way, using certain words, images and formulae,' and this wrong restriction will hinder our prayer and leave our intercession bereft.

5. Awake, O sword, against My Shepherd ... Strike the Shepherd that the sheep may be scattered; and I will turn My hand against the little ones. 'It will come about in all the land,' declares the Lord, 'That two parts in it will be cut off and perish; but the third will be left in it. And I will bring the third part through the fire, refine them as silver is refined, and test them as gold is tested. They will call on My name, and I will answer them; I will say, "They are My people," and they will say, "The Lord is my God"' (Zechariah 13:7–9).

If we are going to be intercessors in order to open up fountains, we will, no doubt, be misunderstood. We will always be under the pressure that the enemy will use to try to destroy the church of God. This is the place of learning how to abide in the cross. The enemy tries to get rid of us, even to tempting us to give up our ministry or to cease our praying because the pressure is so great. To be under such an assault is always to endure a time of smallness and pain. It is a place of threat and challenge. We are bound to enter into such a place if we come to intercession and start to pray to see the enemy's power removed so that the flow of the Spirit can be released, claiming the land for the Lord Jesus.

Let us move to the book of Isaiah.

1. Isaiah 53:12 uses the word *paga*, which is quite rightly interpreted as 'intercession', but has the root idea of 'falling' or 'striking' combined with an indication of strength, energy, resistance and pushing through. 'I will allot Him a portion with the great, and He will divide the booty with the strong; because He poured out Himself to death, and was numbered with the transgressors; yet He Himself bore the sin of many, and interceded for the transgressors.'

2. The death, resurrection and ascension of our Lord Jesus Christ are foretold in Isaiah 52:13: 'Behold, My servant will prosper, He will be high and lifted up and greatly exalted.' This is this exalted position that 'despoils' the enemy and divides the spoils among the Lord's mighty ones (Isaiah 53:12). This passage is used in the New Testament when Jesus talks about binding the strong man (Mark 3:27) – intercession!

3. The Lord is doing this on our behalf because we did not do it for ourselves (Isaiah 59:15–21). This passage tells us God had been looking for a man to intercede, but finding none, he determined to come himself instead.

    From Isaiah chapter 59 right through 60 all the teaching is New Testament teaching. It is all about the church.

It is full of the Holy Spirit. That Spirit is essential for us if we are going to understand God's purposes for us as his people. In Ephesians 6:17 we are told to 'Put on the helmet of salvation' and in verse 14 'the breastplate of righteousness'. Here is Pentecost; the Spirit that is on Jesus is being put on us, and that Spirit is essential for us if we want to co-operate with God and intercede. The armour that we are to put on is not our armour, nor is it the church's armour – it is God's armour! We need it because intercession is a fighting business, and besides, we are now his body.

The God who intervened on our behalf alone is now intervening on behalf of the world that the glory of God may be 'from the rising of the sun even to its setting' (Malachi 1:11). This is being accomplished by the Spirit of the Lord being poured out and by the church taking up the role of interceding and intervening. 'Stand firm', says Ephesians 6:13–14, 'take up the full armor of God, so that you will be able to resist in the evil day, and having done everything, to stand firm.' We are struggling against the rulers and the powers of darkness in the heavenly places. 'And take the helmet of salvation, and the sword of the Spirit, which is the word of God. With all prayer and petition pray at all times in the Spirit' (verses 17–18). Paul put on shoes of evangelism (verse 15) and preached the gospel, opening his mouth with boldness. It is in that context of evangelism that he encouraged us to take the sword of the Spirit and to put on the full armour of God, through all prayer and supplication in the Spirit, in order that we may wrestle, before God, in prayer. Spiritual warfare and prophetic praying are done by those who are engaging the enemy through their ongoing evangelism.

High praises

The phrase that I want us to look at finally is 'high praises'. This is a rare term that has become popular recently. Most churches have by now got out of the habit of thinking that worship is boring, although I am sure that there must be Christians of my generation who remember the time when worship did not really 'turn us on'. A good Wesleyan hymn came up occasionally and then we could really let ourselves go and put our hearts into it, but mostly we were all waiting for the sermon to hear some good preaching. God has been working on his church in recent years and by his Spirit has brought these issues to the fore. He has changed our attitude to worship. He has made us see that worshipping him is the most exciting, fulfilling thing that we can do on earth. But what is 'high praise'? Loving God in worship is one thing, but what does 'high praise' mean?

If we turn to Psalm 149 we will see the word actually used: 'Let the high praises of God be in their mouth, and a two-edged sword in their hand.' High praises are intimately linked to warfare. Worship is not only giving love to God – *high praises* can begin to turn the enemy to flight. High praises are called 'high praises' for many reasons. I will just mention a few.

In Psalm 148 the people of God call upon the heavens to sing and praise the Lord, and then they turn to the angels of heaven and say, 'Praise Him, all His angels.' Then they turn to the earth and say:

> Praise the Lord from the earth! ... Kings of the earth and all peoples; princes and all judges of the earth; both young men and virgins; old men and children. Let them praise the name of the Lord, for His name alone is exalted; His glory is above earth and heaven (verses 11–13).

There is a place for the people of God to instruct and teach the heavens (Ephesians 3:10). In all other places, principalities and powers are negative in their attitude to God so at least some, if not all, are negative here too. The angels are looking down at the church of Christ, watching the body of God's people in whom Jesus lives. And as they look at us they learn, they understand more about the ways of God, and indeed they are driven to praise God, for they do not know him as we know him. We declare Jesus as the Redeemer, as the God of love who has given his son on the cross, even unto death. We declare him as the one who has wiped our souls clean with his own body as it hung on the tree at Calvary. When we 'tell forth his praises' we declare them so that the angels can learn them and join in the song. 'High praise' means that heaven is singing and praising along with the people of God, and that, in turn, releases supernatural activity into the earth. We begin to find that the demonic forces have to fall away at the activity of the saints, which unleashes the supernatural forces. I believe that as this age moves nearer to the coming of our Lord the church of Christ is re-discovering how to move the heavens by its high praises so that God's power might flood out into all the areas of Satan's evil activities and so that he might be put to flight as God's people move forward!

Seoul, South Korea, is home to one of the largest churches in the world. There are many other large churches in that city, numbering hundreds of thousands of believers. The minister of one Presbyterian church there made this statement: 'Anyone who comes to South Korea now will find that their ministry is owned and blessed by God – even if they only have a very mediocre one!' I believe this is because the supernatural powers have been shifted by the praise and intercession of those Korean Christians who spend days on their 'prayer mountains', prayer centres where people praise and worship and make high praises continually, reaching into the heavens and changing the heavenly atmosphere. So much so that the earth has to change very fast to get into line with what is happening in the heavens. Materialism, atheism, rationalism, every aspect of twenty-first-century culture has tried to deflect the church from its true spirit-ual heritage. It does not matter much which things we try to deal with and handle on earth. What matters is whether we are touching the heavens. Are we influencing the supernatural? Are we making spiritual changes? When we do, not only do our spirits rejoice in God, but things also start to happen on earth. We have got to learn how to 'praise high' with the angelic hosts and so find the forces of evil retreating from the terrific grip that they have on so many places in the world.

Psalm 149:5 says: 'Let the godly ones exult in glory; let them sing for joy on their beds.' I think that their 'beds' (or couches) are probably where they recline to eat. The context is festive, and every particle of their being is taken up in worship, the praises of God are sung. Of course, you can put your head down on your pillow and praise God that way too, but it is as we worship that we take up his word, the two-edged sword, and exert it into the earth. We 'execute vengeance', we 'exert judgement' – how did that happen? Well, prison doors were opened and there was confusion in the politics of the day as God moved, by his Spirit, through his people. There were times when God's wrath was felt by people and vengeance was known, as with Ananias and Sapphira (Acts 5:1–11). God was heavy on souls as the church came with high praises on its lips, exerting power and vengeance in the earth and executing his judgement. Jesus said as he rode into Jerusalem to die: 'Now judgment is upon this world; now the ruler of this world will be cast out' (John 12:31). With high praises on our lips and God's word in our hands we proclaim the word of the truth of the cross and we exert the blood of Jesus as we go in to our workplace, down our streets, into our factories, and back to our homes and friends. We demand in the name of the Lord that those situations yield to Jesus' name and give up the grip that Satan has held on them for so long. Here is an active, aggressive church going into battle, exerting the name and blood and the authority of Jesus that overcomes Satan. By 'the blood of the Lamb and because of the word of their testimony, and they did not love their life even when faced with death' (Revelation 12:11). A church that is going to do this is a church that is giving high praise: powerful, intensive praise and prayer, coming from where

Christ is in the heavenly places, where the victory has already been secured, and exerting that victory into earth.

High praise is also mentioned in Psalm 66. It is not apparent in most translations, but it is there in the Hebrew – 'I cried to Him with my mouth, and He was extolled with my tongue' says the psalmist in verse 17. The word 'extolled' is the verbal form of the word for 'high praise'. Verse 18 continues: 'If I regard wickedness in my heart, the Lord will not hear.' High praise on the tongue can be released if we will speak it out, and it has the capacity to lift us when our hearts are weighed down with the iniquity hidden in them. It has the capacity to uncover the iniquity, to dismiss it and to lift our hearts up. The man who said 'If I hide iniquity in my heart the Lord will not hear me' said also after praising the Lord 'My prayer was answered!' He 'high praised' his way right into God's heart!

You will find that when you are among people who are praising God in intensity and power sin begins to be revealed. Deep down, the Lord will show you if you are hiding iniquity in your heart. High praise will lift us high up so that God can hear us and put us where Jesus has provided that we should be – right there where he is, seated in the heavenly places in him (Ephesians 2:6). We should not have to keep saying 'Keep looking up, brother!' as an encouragement: we should say 'Keep looking down!' We could and should be already up there, through high praise, in the 'throne room'. We are going to exert the authority we find there to the ends of the earth and then Jesus will come!

Let us praise the Lord with high praises and move into action in these last days so that we see the world fall into the hand of our God and the kingdom of this world become the kingdom of our God and of his Christ (Revelation 11:15).